ON SUICIDE BOMBING

THE WELLEK LECTURES

PREVIOUSLY PUBLISHED WELLEK LIBRARY LECTURES

Harold Bloom   *The Breaking of the Vessels*
Perry Anderson   *In the Tracks of Historical Materialism*
Frank Kermode   *Forms of Attention*
Jacques Derrida   *Memoires for Paul de Man*
J. Hillis Miller   *The Ethics of Reading*
Jean-François Lyotard   *Peregrinations: Law, Form, Event*
Murray Krieger   *Reopening of Closure: Organicism Against Itself*
Edward W. Said   *Musical Elaborations*
Hélène Cixous   *Three Steps on the Ladder of Writing*
Fredric Jameson   *The Seeds of Time*
Evelyn Fox Keller   *Refiguring Life: Metaphors of Twentieth-Century
                                Biology*
Geoffrey Hartman   *A Fateful Question of Culture*
Wolfgang Iser   *The Range of Interpretation*
Harry Harootunian   *History's Disquiet: Modernity and Everyday Life*
Judith Butler   *Antigone's Claim: Kinship Between Life and Death*
Jean Baudrillard   *The Vital Illusion*
Gayatri Chakravorty Spivak   *Death of a Discipline*
Paul Gilroy   *Postcolonial Melancholia*

ON
SUICIDE BOMBING

TALAL ASAD

COLUMBIA UNIVERSITY PRESS | NEW YORK

COLUMBIA UNIVERSITY PRESS
Publishers Since 1893

New York   Chichester, West Sussex
Copyright © 2007 Columbia University Press

Library of Congress Cataloging-in-Publication Data

Asad, Talal.
On suicide bombing / Talal Asad.
p. cm.
Includes bibliographical references.
ISBN 978-0-231-14152-9 (clothbound : alk. paper) —
ISBN 978-0-231-51197-1 (ebooks)
1. Terrorism.   2. Terrorism—Psychological aspects.   3. Terrorism—Religious aspects—Islam.   4. Suicide bombers—Psychology.   5. Victims of terrorism—Psychology.   I. Title.

HV6431.A82 2007
363.325—DC22
2006030533

DESIGNED BY VIN DANG

c 10 9 8 7 6 5 4

p 10 9 8 7 6 5 4 3 2 1

EDITORIAL NOTE

The Wellek Library Lectures in Critical Theory are given annually at the University of California, Irvine, under the auspices of the Critical Theory Institute. The following lectures were given in May 2006

THE CRITICAL THEORY INSTITUTE
John H. Smith, *Director*

CONTENTS

ON SUICIDE BOMBING

INTRODUCTION

LIKE MOST NEW YORKERS who were in the city on September 11, 2001, I encountered the events of that day largely through the media, through the pall of smoke that hung over the south of the island, and through the emotion infusing the conversation and demeanor of ordinary Americans. For many Muslims living in the United States, September 11 was the beginning of a long period of anxiety, during which they found themselves associated, occasionally explicitly but more often implicitly, with terrorism.[1] For many non-Muslims in the United States, Western Europe, and Israel, the suicide bomber quickly became the icon of an Islamic "culture of death."[2] This led me to try to think in a sustained way about the contemporary mode of violence that is described by much of the Western media as "Islamic terrorism." Is there, I asked myself, a religiously motivated terrorism? If so, how does it differ from other cruelties? What makes its motivation—as opposed to the simple intent to kill—religious? Where does it stand in relation to other forms of collective violence? How is the image of the suicide bomber, bringing death to himself and others, addressed by Christians and post-Christians? My questions, I stress, arose not primarily from ethical concerns but from a curiosity about conceptual and material connections. Thinking about suicide bombing, in its banality and its horror, was for me a way of opening up some modern assumptions about dying and killing. The general thought I have pursued is that however much we try to distinguish between morally good and morally evil ways of killing, our attempts are beset with contradictions, and these contradictions remain a fragile part of our modern subjectivity.

My focus on the United States and Israel in this book is deliberate. There is terrorism in other places, of course: Sri Lanka, India, Indonesia, Russia, to name only a few countries. And the United States has long had its homegrown, institutionalized terror, although this is not what people today remember when they refer to terrorism.[3] Nevertheless, the idea of a war on terror is uniquely developed and expressed in a particular place—the United States—and most of the theorization about terrorism (and about just war) occurs there, as well as in Europe and Israel. I am not interested in providing a representative—let alone a comprehensive—survey of terrorism as a unique phenomenon of our time. Put simply, I argue that the creation of terror and the perpetration of atrocities are aspects of militant action in the unequal world we inhabit, of our notions of what is cruel and what is necessary, and of the emotions with which we justify or condemn particular acts of death dealing.

The book itself has a simple structure. In the first chapter, I begin by examining the "clash of civilizations" thesis that purports to explain contemporary Islamic jihadism as the essence of contemporary terrorism, and I argue against the kind of history that assumes self-contained civilizations having fixed values. I then discuss the attempt by a distinguished philosopher to differentiate just war from terrorism, and I speculate on the reasons for the prominence of a public discourse on terror. Terrorism, I point out, is an epistemological object in modern society, something that calls for theorization (what is terrorism?) as well as for practical information gathering (how can one forestall this danger?). These two tasks are dependent on each other. Terrorism, however, is more than the object of these tasks. It is also an integral part of liberal subjectivities (the urge to defeat political terror, the fear of social vulnerability, the horror and fascination with death and destruction), although terror itself is dismissed as being essentially part of a nonmodern, nonliberal culture. In the second chapter, I look critically at a range of current explanations of suicide terrorism that are now being put forward, and I question the preoccupation by writers on the subject with attributing distinctive motives (as opposed to the manifest intention to kill) to perpetrators of suicide bombing. I say that motives in general are more complicated than is popularly supposed and that the assumption that they are truths to be accessed is mistaken: the motives of suicide bombers in particular are inevitably fictions that justify our responses but that we cannot verify. I then move away from writers attempting to explain the phenomenon of suicide bombings who address larger questions of killing and dying in relation to politics. Drawing on the history of ideas, I emphasize that although liberal thought separates the idea of violence from the idea of politics, mortal violence is integral to liberalism as a political formation. More significantly, I suggest that legitimate violence exercised in and by the modern progressive state—including the liberal democratic state—possesses a peculiar character that is absent in terrorist violence (absent not because of the latter's virtue but because of the former's capability): a combination of cruelty and compassion that sophisticated social institutions enable and encourage. In the third and last chapter, I explore the idea of horror as a common reaction to suicide and especially to suicide bombing. On the one hand, I turn to anthropological writing to elaborate the notion that horror has to do with the collapse of social and personal identity and thus with the dissolution of form. On the other hand, I draw on some aspects of Christian theology: the crucifixion is the most famous suicide in history, whose horror is transmuted into the project of redeeming universal humanity—again, through a combination of cruelty and compassion. This is the most speculative part of the book, but it is essential to the layered account I finally offer of what horror at suicide bombing consists in.

A brief warning against a possible misreading of this book: I do *not* plead that terrorist atrocities may sometimes be morally justified. I am simply impressed by the fact that modern states are able to destroy and disrupt life more easily and on a much grander scale than ever before and that terrorists cannot reach this capability. I am also struck by the ingenuity with which so many politicians, public intellectuals, and journalists provide moral justifications for killing and demeaning other human beings. What seems to matter is not the killing and dehumanization as such but how one kills and with what motive. People at all times have, of course, justified the killing of so-called enemies and others they deem not deserving to live. The only difference is that today liberals who engage in this justification think they are different because morally advanced. That very thought has social implications, and it is therefore that thought that makes a real difference. Liberal thought begins from the notion that everyone has the absolute right to defend himself, in the full knowledge that the idea of defense is subject to considerable interpretation, so that (for example) liberation from the oppressor in Iraq becomes part of defense for both the American occupier and the insurgency. Many liberals also believe that people have a moral obligation to attack evil, either in order to redeem themselves or to redeem others who cannot do so for themselves. The notion of evil is not conceived of as a principle essential to the world—as in Manichaean and Zoroastrian teaching—but as a dynamic principle that opposes divine will and is therefore eliminable. Consequently, it is resistance to that will that defines evil, and all virtuous men are urged to overcome it at any cost. (According to Christian belief, Christ triumphed over evil, God reconciled the world to himself, by the crucifixion.)[4] Fighting evil is, of course, an old justification, but it often finds new formulations today. I do not mean by this that today's modern world is, as many hold, simply an unfolding of Christianity. In my view there are continuities and also crucial ruptures between secular modernity and its past.

Finally, this book does not pretend to offer solutions to moral dilemmas about institutionalized violence. It makes no case for accepting some kinds of cruelty as opposed to others. Its hope, rather, is to disturb the reader sufficiently that he or she will be able to take a distance from the complacent public discourse that prepackages moral responses to terrorism, war, and suicide bombing.

The following chapters were first given as the Wellek Library lectures at the University of California, Irvine, on May 15–17, 2006. I am grateful to the Institute for Critical Theory for inviting me to deliver them, to the audience for their questions and comments, and especially to John H. Smith, Director of the Institute, for his hospitality. My thanks also to other members of the Institute—especially Gabriela Schwab, Inderpal Grewal, and Bill Maurer, who welcomed me generously. A number of friends and colleagues have offered helpful comments on various drafts: Hussein Agrama, Partha Chatterjee, Veena Das, Maria Pia Di Bella, Abou Farman, Jeffrey Goldfarb, Baber Johansen, Mahmood Mamdani, Tomaz Mastnak, Keith Nield, Gyan Pandey, David Scott, Mohammed Tabishat, and David Wolton. None of them, of course, is responsible for the opinions I have expressed here.

TERRORISM

ON THE EVENING of the attack on the World Trade Center and the Pentagon, President Bush made a statement in his address to the nation:

> Good evening. Today, our fellow citizens, our way of life, our very freedom came under attack in a series of deliberate and deadly *terrorist acts*. The victims were in airplanes, or in their offices; secretaries, businessmen and women, military and federal workers; moms and dads, friends and neighbors. Thousands of lives were suddenly ended by evil, despicable *acts of terror*. The pictures of airplanes flying into buildings, fires burning, huge structures collapsing, have filled us with disbelief, terrible sadness, and a quiet, unyielding anger. The *acts of mass murder* were intended to frighten our nation into chaos and retreat. But they have failed; our country is strong.[1]

The next day, Mr. Bush opened with another statement: "I have just completed a meeting with my national security team, and we have received the latest intelligence updates. The deliberate and deadly attacks which were carried out yesterday against our country were *more than acts of terror*. They were *acts of war*. This will require our country to unite in steadfast determination and resolve."[2] Later, both the Bush administration and the U.S. media fixed on the phrase War Against Terrorism (or Terror).

Many commentators asked why the deployment of organized violence against terrorism was being described as a war. Among those skeptical of this usage was Alain Badiou, who made the obvious point that in the past, when governments responded to terrorism—especially in the context of colonialism—they spoke not of war but of police action. Governments that had had to deal with the Baader-Meinhof group in Germany, the IRA in Britain, ETA in Spain, or the Red Brigade in Italy, typically described their responses as "security measures" or "police actions," rather than using the term "war." Badiou proposed that in its capacity as a world power the United States had privileged war as the sign of its presence. From the beginning, he said, its political formation was achieved through a long history of military encounters across the North American continent and abroad.[3]

I want to take up the other half of the question, however: why is the term "terrorism" so prominent today when talking about certain kinds of contemporary violence—not only in the United States but also in Europe, Israel, and other parts of the world? One suggestion has been that the previous violent groups in Europe were all operating within the framework of the nation-state and were therefore insiders; the present adversaries (Muslim terrorists) are outsiders—even when they are citizens of the liberal democratic state or inhabitants of its governed territories. On the other hand, however reprehensible it was to liberals, the violence of Marxists and nationalists was understandable in terms of progressive, secular history. The violence of Islamic groups, on the other hand, is incomprehensible to many precisely because it is not embedded in a historical narrative—history in the "proper" sense. As the violence of what is often referred to as a totalitarian religious tradition hostile to democratic politics, it is seen to be irrational as well as being an international threat.

The last written statements of the leading attacker against the World Trade Center apparently contained Islamic themes. Religion was therefore a favorite explanation of what had happened, and the stream of articles and television programs grew, claiming to lay bare the Islamic roots of terrorism. The religious ideology behind terrorism that virtually everyone would come to hear about was *jihād*, described by university professors and journalists as the Islamic concept of holy war against the infidel. The Anglo-American orientalist Bernard Lewis popularized this view as a "clash of civilizations." In the first, conquering phase of Islamic history—wrote Lewis—the organized violence called *jihād* was a culturally distinctive expression of Muslim intolerance and arrogance towards non-Muslims. Subsequently, with the decline of Islamic civilization and the triumph of the West, Islamist violence came to represent a fanatical resentment against modernity. Many commentators who have followed this line of thought have insisted that unless and until the Islamic world is radically reformed, the extreme danger of terrorism in our so-called age of jihadism will remain.

Yet another—more complicated—story can be told, one that doesn't lend itself so easily to the popular drama of a clash of civilizations.

It is rarely noted in polemical accounts that for many centuries after the early conquests the majority of the populations in countries with Muslim rulers remained Christian, active as such in many spheres of public life, and that therefore public institutions and practices in the early Muslim empire were largely continuous with the Christian societies it incorporated. Indeed, in crucial respects, the Islamic empire was the inheritor of Byzantium, and the histories of both sides of the Mediterranean have always been intertwined through the exchange of ideas, practices, and commodities. It is true that in the earlier centuries Muslim armies penetrated Christian lands, but at first the European Christians did not regard the battles between themselves and Muslims as expressions of a cosmic struggle between good and evil.[4] It was only with the Crusades that the papacy promoted the ideology of a unified Christendom at war with a unified Islam. These were the first militant incursions of

European Christians into Muslim lands, and some centuries later they culminated in the great European empires of the nineteenth and twentieth centuries. The histories of Europe and Islam cannot be completely separated.

The trouble with the clash of civilizations talk is not simply that it ignores a rich history of mutual borrowings and continuous interactions among Christians, Jews, and Muslims. It is that the very identity of a people as European (or Islamic) depends on the definition of a selective civilizational heritage of which most of the people to whom it is attributed are in fact almost completely ignorant—a heritage with which even individual members of the elite (the civilization's guardians) are only incompletely familiar. This legitimizes the internal inequality of those embraced by the civilization as well as their difference from other peoples. In other words, it is not simply that a heritage is invariably selective; it is that the people are defined by the civilization that is supposed to be their heritage. And yet, sociologically, the people who are said to belong to that civilization are highly differentiated by class and region and gender.

All histories are selective, of course, but what they leave out and how they interpret what they select are more interesting than the mere fact of selection. Thus when polemicists speak of Christianity as the essential core of Western civilization—or the origin of modern democracy—they do not have in mind the Orthodox churches of Eastern Europe or the ancient Christian congregations of the Middle East. And yet central doctrines of Christianity (the Trinity, Atonement, etc.) as well as major institutions (monasticism) first emerged there and not in Latin Christendom. This leaves it unclear as to whether talk about Christianity as the essential midwife of our modern secular world ("the point where, thanks to religion, a society with no further need for religion arises," as Marcel Gauchet puts it)[5] is to be understood as a theological argument or a sociological one.

In Western histories of Islam, *jihād* has been a central theme, although in Islamic thought *jihād* is not a central notion. Nevertheless, it has been compared by Western historians to the medieval

Christian concept of the Crusade. The only difference, we are given to understand, is that while the Crusade is no longer part of Western modernity, *jihād* is integral to an Islamic civilization that is largely rooted in religion. But the differences are more complicated than this civilizational contrast would suggest. To begin with, the theory and practice of the Crusade were closely connected with the rise of the papal monarchy (and afterward with the sacralization of territorially based kingship), and there is no parallel story for the Muslim world in the case of *jihād*. The Arabic word for "holy," *muqaddas*, is never applied to "war," *harb*, in the classical texts. And because there has never been a centralized theological authority in the Islamic world, there was never a consensus about the virtue of religious warfare. Thus in the first two centuries of Islamic history jurists residing close to the revered sites of Islam (in Mecca and Medina) had a different view from those who lived in Damascus and Baghdad, the successive imperial capitals. The former maintained that the pursuit of *jihād* (and even stationing oneself in military camps at the frontier far from the original centers of Islam) was not an obligatory duty for all Muslims, that there was merely a requirement that some Muslims undertake the defense of Islamic territory, and that in any case other religious acts had greater merit. In later centuries the legal theory of *jihād* came to be articulated in the context of a distinction between *dār ul-harb* (the domain of war) and *dār ul-Islām* (the domain of peace) making *jihād* appropriate only to the former. Of course, this theory didn't prevent Muslim rulers from waging war on one another in the domain of peace or from making treaties with Christian neighbors. Muslims fought Muslims, sometimes with Christian allies. But legal categories other than the ones I have mentioned were employed to legitimize or condemn such conflicts.

Islamic debates on this subject, in which jurists belonging to the different schools engaged one another, evolved in complex relation to historical events. The legal ideas put forward in these arguments cannot be reduced to the simple doctrinal binary (unremitting distance from and hostility toward all non-Muslims, unqualified solidarity among and loyalty to all Muslims) that recent polemical writing in the West has made familiar. From very early on, another juridical category was established, called *dār ul-'ahd* (the domain of treaties), that allowed for peaceful trade and social intercourse between Muslim and non-Muslim territories. Most premodern Islamic jurists ruled that it was fully permissible according to the *sharī'a* (the religious law) for Muslims to live as subjects to a Christian prince (as in Spain), so long as they were able to practice Islam openly. The Ottoman Empire alone made a succession of treaties with Christian powers over the centuries that allowed European merchants to establish themselves within imperial lands with extraterritorial privileges. (The social situation of ordinary non-Muslim subjects within Muslim-majority countries varied at different times and in different places, but in general it tended to worsen when outsiders attacked Muslims.)[6]

In colonial times, a further reformulation of the doctrine of *jihād* took place: Muslims living under a non-Muslim government (and therefore technically in *dār ul-harb*) were not to undertake *jihād* as long as they were able to practice Islam and allowed to maintain its central institutions. Nevertheless, Muslim rebels against colonial regimes sometimes invoked *jihād*, and in recent years militant Islamists have raised *jihād* to the level of an individual religious duty (*fard al-'ayn*). But such usages have not had the support of most Muslim jurists, for the legal preconditions of *jihād*—it has been argued by Muslim scholars—must include both the presence of a genuine threat to Islam and the likelihood of success in opposing it. Terms like *jihād*, *dār ul-harb* and *dār ul-Islām* are therefore not parts of a transhistorical worldview; they belong to an elaborate political-theological vocabulary in which jurists, men of religious learning, and modernist reformers debated and polemicized in response to varying circumstances.

In brief, there is no such thing as a clash of civilizations because there are no self-contained societies to which fixed civilizational values correspond. On the contrary, the penetration of European economic, political, and ideological powers in the Middle East—especially since the beginning of the nineteenth century—led to many practices being changed. European states conducted their strategic and commercial rivalries throughout the lands of a weakened—and eventually a broken-up—Ottoman Empire, building and controlling transport systems (the Suez Canal being the most important), promising and establishing a national home in Palestine to the Jews, dividing up the Middle East into mandates and spheres of influence, making unequal treaties with sovereign Arab polities, exploiting petroleum resources, and so forth. The United States has simply continued in this interventionist tradition with its own strategic and economic interests in the Middle East and has invoked new justifications for intervention in the present.

My concern, I stress, is not to find culprits but to point to a few of the complicated connections that give us a better picture of contemporary problems in the area that Europeans first called the Middle East. Thus Saddam's cruelties were certainly his own, but the fact that the United States supplied him with vital military intelligence in his aggressive war against Iran and the Europeans helped him manufacture chemical weapons that he used against Iranians as well as Iraqi Kurds complicates the question of culpability—if culpability is to be assigned. Although the French support for the Algerian coup that suppressed the FIS after its electoral victories in 1991 did not determine the subsequent massacres, their support is not unconnected with what followed. Similarly, although the brutalities of the Islamic Republic of Iran are not caused by Western states, the regime's emergence is not unrelated to the CIA coup (supported by Britain) that inaugurated the dictatorship of the shah in the 1950s. And again, Mubarak's political repression and use of torture are not, of course, dictated by U.S. imperialism (although the Bush administration has made use of this skill by proxy), but the war against terror has certainly supplied him and other regimes in the region with greater justification for cruelty. As George Packer so nicely put it in his interesting essay on liberal internationalism: "How can the

U.S. fight jihadism without supporting dictatorships?"[7] In the case of Iraq, however, the United States decided to destroy a dictatorship and dismantle a state for its own reasons. No person who has followed the ensuing events can doubt that the rise in jihadism and the vicious sectarian killings are closely connected with the U.S. invasion and occupation.

In a densely interconnected world—more so than ever before—it is not sensible, in my view, to talk about the overriding need for reform in so-called Islamic civilization without at the same time reappraising the attitudes, institutions, and policies in Western countries. Clearly, if reform is needed in Muslim-majority countries—and reform is certainly being demanded by their populations—it is needed no less in Europe and the United States, *not least in the many ways that their policies impinge on the Middle East.* Yet the idea of autonomous civilizations is difficult to shake.

It is in this connection that one might turn to Richard Rorty's recent worry.[8] Another major attack by terrorists in the West, he fears, would probably spell the end of historical democracy there: "The measures [Western] governments will consider it necessary to impose are likely to bring about the end of many of the sociopolitical institutions that emerged in Europe and North America in the two centuries since the bourgeois revolutions." The connection between external violence and the sociopolitical institutions internal to Western democracy is, however, more complicated than Rorty suggests here. Long ago, Max Weber observed that European forms of freedom and democracy were made possible in part by the forcible expansion of the West over many centuries into the non-European world—and in spite of the simultaneous growth of a standardizing capitalism. This led him to fear that the ending of the West's territorial expansion in which the drive for freedom was deeply embedded would seriously compromise its democracy.[9] Weber did not, of course, foresee the spread of neoliberal capitalism around the globe—largely through the activities of financial institutions internal to today's Western democracy (the IMF, the World Bank, the

U.S. Treasury)—nor its fearful consequences in growing economic inequality and political instability compounded by global warming (aggravated if not caused by disproportionate energy use in the rich, industrially advanced countries). He could not anticipate the serious population dislocation and political instability in the poorer south that now encourage waves of illegal migration toward the north or the alarm and compassion that this would generate in Euro-American countries, leading to repeated calls for further military intervention in the south—to restore political order, to provide humanitarian aid, to punish so-called rogue regimes, to secure energy resources. At any rate, the implications of these tasks for Western democracy are at least as serious as the activities of terrorists, and both together inhabit a space of violence that is far more inclusive than Rorty's account suggests. If Weber's account of Western democracy is at all valid (and I am persuaded that it is), then what one finds is a shift in which the violence that yesterday facilitated freedom at home is today facilitating a creeping unfreedom. I stress that my concern here is not to blame the West but to substitute the idea of a historical space in which violence circulates, in which our wider aims are too often undermined by our own actions, for the simple agentive model that many commentators employ, in which rational democrats in the West react defensively to destructive terrorists from the East.

Critics who argue that the language of the clash of civilizations facilitates the discourse on terrorism are right. But the question remains: why is the term "terrorism" so prominent today? Before attempting an answer to this question, it is necessary to ask another: How is the difference between terrorism and war defined in contemporary public discourse? I begin by looking at some arguments by an eminent political philosopher who has tried to answer this question: Michael Walzer.[10] His most recent book on the distinction between kinds of political killing, *Arguing About War*, is addressed to a wide, educated audience.

Walzer takes it as unproblematic that war is a legal activity when it fulfills certain conditions (e.g., self-defense or fulfilling a treaty obligation toward a state that is attacked). He affirms existing international law (the law of force) that legitimizes certain types of violence and stigmatizes others—even as domestic law does within national boundaries. This immediately makes it quite clear what terrorism is for Walzer: terrorism is not only illegal and therefore morally worse than killing in war; it is worse even than the crime of murder. "This, then," he writes, "is the peculiar evil of terrorism— not only the killing of innocent people but also the intrusion of fear into everyday life, the violation of private purposes, the insecurity of public spaces, the endless coerciveness of precaution."[11] For Walzer, of course, it is not merely the deliberate creation of fear for political purposes that defines terrorism; the killing of innocents is a necessary (though not a sufficient) criterion. What Walzer condemns in war is *excess* and in terrorism its *essence*. States kill, too, of course, although they claim to kill only legitimately. But whether states, unlike terrorists, kill only those who are legitimately killable is partly what the rules of war address.

Walzer doesn't approve of generals who win by ruthless means: "In all times, and in conventional as well as political wars, we ought to require of officers that they attend to the value of civilian lives, and we should refuse to honor officers who fail to do that" (p. 31). Yet, in common with many who have written on this topic, Walzer pays no attention to a curious contradiction at the heart of the liberal West's culture of war to which I shall return later: on the one hand, the state's need to legitimize organized violence against a collective enemy (including civilians) and, on the other, the humanitarian desire to save human lives.[12] To "attend to the value of civilian lives" is more ambiguous than appears at first sight.

It is in this context that Walzer argues for the limited character of the humanitarian principle, for overlooking it in the event of a supreme emergency: "There are moments when the rules can be and perhaps have to be overridden. They have to be overridden precisely because they have not been suspended. And overriding the rules leaves guilt behind, as a recognition of the enormity of what we have done and a commitment not to make our actions into an easy precedent for the future" (p. 34). Now Walzer does not say so, but there is no reason why, in the war against terrorism, this permission cannot cover the use of torture against presumed terrorist captives, on the grounds that, however reprehensible it may be to liberal sensibilities, the extraction of information from the enemy by breaking humanitarian rules is vital to the conduct of such a war.

Like Bernard Lewis, Michael Walzer believes that the cause of terrorism is the failure of Muslim countries to modernize, a failure that explains the scapegoating of the United States and Israel by Muslim immigrants in Western countries and also the spawning of highly dangerous conspiracies among them: "The important battle against terror is being waged right here," he warns, "and in Britain and Germany and Spain, and in other countries of the Arab and Islamic diaspora" (p. 138). Walzer does not discuss what kind of politics might be called for in a time of global crisis and instead supports an extension of the battle against terror into immigrant communities as a priority, making the liberal assumption (which I discuss in my second chapter) that the problem of politics is radically separate from the problem of violence and that it is the primary task of the state to exclude violence from the arena of politics and confine it to the domain of war.

But Walzer wants to reassure his readers. He proposes that a public transgression in the domain of war should (will?) be accompanied by a sense of remorse and that when this happens, the feelings of guilt about what has been done may make it more difficult to repeat that transgression in the future. In this context, guilt is regarded as a sign of grace. The moral drama in which this redemption is played out is familiar to existential philosophy. "A morally strong leader," writes Walzer, "is someone who understands why it is wrong to kill the innocent and refuses to do so, refuses again and again, until the heavens are about to fall. And then he becomes a moral criminal (like Albert Camus's 'just assassin') who knows that he can't do what he has to do—and finally does" (p. 45). How should one understand this tale? Certainly, the leader who has to act like a criminal a second time may do so with a bad conscience, and in greater anguish than before. That is what makes him a "morally strong" leader. If he killed the innocent without a flicker of conscience, he would simply be an immoral criminal. Now, for a Christian who kills unjustly in war, there is the theory of atonement that presupposes a life after death; for a subject who kills unjustly in peace, there is the theory of punishment that presupposes state law. When Walzer speaks of guilt in the context of "a morally strong leader" at war, it is unlikely that he has either of these theories in mind. Guilt here is not a legal judgment but a sensibility.

The morally strong leader can turn, when necessary, to what Walzer calls "emergency ethics." "This is the essential feature of emergency ethics: that we recognize at the same time the evil we oppose and the evil we do, and that we set ourselves, so far as possible, against both" (p. 49). What exactly Walzer intends by the phrase "so far as possible" is not clear. Perhaps it is a vague sense that in a war against an unjust enemy, one cannot condemn the use of any available weapon as strongly as one condemns the evil that confronts one without risking a wrong choice. But if the phrase "as far as possible" is intended to nudge the just warrior in the right direction, isn't Walzer's claim about the equal rejection of two evils brought into question? If the moral scruple he endorses must never be strong enough to inhibit successfully the use of evil means when necessary, is there any need for it to be present at all?

What is it precisely that allows the leaders of a political community to confront a potential evil by doing evil? According to Walzer, it is the protection of the community itself. "Not, I want to stress, of the state," he observes, "the state is nothing more than an instrument of the community, a particular structure for organizing collective action that can always be replaced by some other structure. The political community (the community of faith too) can't be similarly replaced. It consists of men, women, and children living in a certain way, its replacement would require either the elimination of the people *or the coercive transformation of their way of life*. Neither of these actions is morally acceptable" (p. 49, my emphasis). In those situations, says Walzer, we may act immorally—but "only at the last minute and under absolute necessity" (p. 50). I'll return shortly to this idea, but first I want to ask whether the license to kill can be separated so casually from the state. The modern state is not, after all, simply an instrument of the community. It is an autonomous structure that regulates, represents, and protects a community of citizens. The state authorizes the killing of human beings, demands the ultimate sacrifice of its citizens when they are at war. It seeks to maintain the correct demographic character and the desired territorial extent for the community that is its object.

Walzer's virtual dismissal of the state at this point is curious because his overall argument is essentially state-oriented. Thus he insists that the militant who carries out acts of terror against civilians is never faced by the "last resort" and he is therefore not coerced. It is precisely a quality of the terrorist that he moves precipitately to death dealing as a political means. "It is not so easy to reach the 'last resort,'" says Walzer. "To get there one must indeed try everything (which is a lot of things) and not just once... Politics is the art of repetition" (p. 53). But then why doesn't this observation apply to the state that launches a war? In the case of war, Walzer is reluctant to apply the stringent conditions he imposes on the militant. He pleads that by demanding that war be declared only as a last resort, one is in effect making it impossible to declare war, because "we can never reach lastness, or we can never know that we have reached it. There is always something else to do: another diplomatic note, another United Nations resolution, another meeting" (p. 88). Walzer is right. But how does this plea for decisiveness on the part of the state on the verge of war relate to his strictures against terrorist violence on the grounds that the would-be terrorist can never claim to have reached the limit? Is it plausible to assume—as Walzer evidently does—that the possibility of liberal politics is always a given? Thus the recently elected Hamas government in occupied Palestine will not be allowed by the United States, Israel, and the European Union to practice "the art of repetition," and the reason given for this is not that Hamas does not recognize democratic politics but that it does not recognize Israel.

Unlike Walzer, I am not interested here in the question, "When are particular acts of violence to be condemned as evil, and what are the moral limits to justified counterviolence?" I am trying to think instead about the following question: "What does the adoption of particular definitions of death dealing do to military conduct in the world?" For example, if state killing is authorized on the basis of due proportionality and military necessity (as humanitarian law requires of conduct in war), and if the question of what is proportional or necessary cannot be determined without regard to overall war aims as well as military strategy (there are always war aims in every war), every kind of forceful means can be—and is—used in war on that basis, including the destruction of civilians and the terrorizing of entire populations.

International law specialist David Kennedy has written a searching study of the ways in which humanitarian policy making blends into the strategic logic of warfare—although he remains, in the end, surprisingly optimistic. At one point, speaking of state violence, he observes:

> We can easily call to mind historical examples of "wanton violence" in war. And of course they have sometimes been sanctioned by military leadership. But rare is the commander who orders "unnecessary" "wanton violence" "disproportional" to any legitimate military objective. Far more often the tactics employed by *other* forces will seem excessive. The vocabulary in which this charge is made, and defended, is the vocabulary of humanitarian law. Indeed, whatever tactics seem extreme—carpet bombing, siege, nuclear first use, suicide bombing, terrorizing the civilian population—the condemnation and the

defense seem to converge on the vocabulary of necessity, proportionality, and so forth. Think of Hiroshima.[13]

Kennedy is right about the humanitarian vocabulary of necessity,
proportionality, and humanity that is now commonly used in arguments over particular events in war in the attempt to subject
military conduct to transcendent rules. But it is worth bearing in
mind that terrorists themselves often talk about what they do in
the language of necessity and humanity. The Red Brigades in 1970s
Italy, for example, mirrored the judicial authority of the state and
challenged its monopoly of violence, trying kidnapped victims for
crimes against the people and then executing them. Such acts not
only transcend the limits of (state) law in the name of revolutionary justice, they do so by explicitly invoking a wider humanity. Thus
when the Italian prime minister was kidnapped and killed, the incident was described by a Red Brigade ideologist as "the highest act of
humanity possible in this class-divided society"[14] and therefore as
necessary. The ruthlessness of terrorists often matches the effects
achieved in the strategic strikes made by state armies, even when
the latter use the language of humanitarian law in which a liberating or self-defensive purpose can be claimed.

Pointing out that the new law of force is a field of argument rather
than a set of absolute rules (e.g., civilians must not be harmed), Kennedy suggests that the consequent flexibility makes for an advance
on the previous position. I would suggest, however, that the sense
that this constitutes an advance may be connected to the increased
importance given to the sovereignty of individual conscience in this
matter. Law is always a matter of argument because it requires interpretation, but here emphasis is placed not so much on what the
military commander *does* (which is comparatively easy to determine
in relation to absolute rules) but on *what he has judged necessary and
then chosen to do*, an interpretive process that lies at the heart of
modern ethics. And yet what matters primarily here is not a vocabulary of moral argument or the conscience of the virtuous warrior but

the existence of an independent institutional structure that has the ability to set a legal process into motion and apply its legal verdict in relation to conduct in war regardless of who is to be judged. But it is a banal fact that powerful states are never held accountable to such institutions, that only the weak and the defeated can be convicted of war crimes and crimes against humanity.

Walzer is adamant that, unlike the aerial bombing of German civilians during World War II, suicide bombing is terrorism and that, as terrorism, it is an evil in need not of analysis and understanding but of moral condemnation and firm practical response. Particular wars may be unjustly declared, wars may sometimes use immoral means and be concluded in a vindictive way, but wars as such are not in principle immoral. Terrorism, on the other hand, is always and in principle evil. Thus the definition of war and terrorism as opposites makes it possible to speak of a war *on* terror and to assume that the state can conduct itself freely toward the terrorist precisely because he does not respect the law.

Walzer's fundamental concern throughout his book is to articulate and clarify his moral intuitions rather than to question and analyze them. Thus he believes that terrorist operations in Israel are a product of evil (exactly like those of al-Qaeda against the West) because they are part of the Palestinian war to destroy a sovereign political community. The assaults of the Israeli army and airforce in the West Bank and Gaza are therefore to be seen as preemptive self-defense and thus in principle as just war. Walzer's account of the Palestine/Israel conflict provides, I think, a central example of how some liberal intellectuals conceive of the difference between war and terrorism. The century-long history of the conflict (expansion on the one side, dispossession on the other) is set aside, and attention is directed instead at present feelings. "For all their military strength, Israelis feel terribly vulnerable" (p. 108), Walzer observes, whereas "for the Palestinians, the years of occupation have been [felt as] years of disgrace" (p. 107). Walzer doesn't hesitate to convey his own feelings about the settlements that he thinks make peace with

Palestinians difficult: "the [Jewish] settler movement is the function-
al equivalent of the [Palestinian] terrorist organizations. I hasten to
add that it is *not the moral equivalent*. The settlers are not murderers,
even if there are a number of terrorists among them" (p. 119, italics
in original). The haste and emphasis with which this point is made
reveals some of the feelings behind the notion of terrorism: proud
identification with a flourishing political community—a liberal democracy—and with its military and economic successes and a fear
for its safety. What this rhetorical move does, of course, is to pro-
hibit the use of the appellation "terrorist" for the Israeli settlers and
to invest the Israeli army with the aura of defenders engaged in a
just war against Palestinian terrorists.

This is made formally explicit in Walzer's classification of the
conflict into four concurrent wars: "The first is a Palestinian war to
destroy the state of Israel. The second is a Palestinian war to create
an independent state alongside Israel, ending the occupation of the
West Bank and Gaza. The third is an Israeli war for the security of
Israel within the 1967 borders. The fourth is an Israeli war for Greater Israel, for the settlements and the occupied territories" (p. 113).
This simple classification presents readers with a balance between
the two sides—terrorists/extremists on one side and protagonists of
just war on the other—a political and moral equivalence between
occupier and occupied. One can recount the story of conflict in a
different way, however: there is a single unequal struggle (not four
wars) stretching over at least sixty years in which each side has pursued different strategies and rhetoric at different times that have
not met with equal success. Thus the distinction between the third
"war" (for the settlements) and the fourth (for the security of Israel)
is not as clear-cut as Walzer's classification suggests, because, on
the one hand, virtually no significant Israeli political party is prepared to return conquered East Jerusalem and all its surrounding
settlements and, on the other hand, arguments for Israel's security
are closely bound up with claims to large parts of occupied Palestine, which accounts for the widespread popularity in Israel of what

is known there as "disengagement"—whose visible symbol is the wall. It is not clear how far disengagement is related to a sense of desperation and how far to a desire not to be seen to be ruling over a non-Jewish majority, but it has certainly been successful in isolating the Palestinian population geographically and politically.

What is evident is that the feeling of vulnerability among Israelis and their supporters is not equivalent to the objective gains (territorial, military, economic, cultural, etc.) that the Jews have made in Palestine over a century. By this, I don't mean to say that Israeli feelings should be dismissed or that they are insignificant but simply that the two are literally incomparable. Indeed, the reality of such feelings, their importance, must be recognized. How that feeling of vulnerability has been achieved is, of course, another matter, because it is rooted not in an evaluation of contemporary Palestinian power but in a collective trauma resulting from genocide—perpetrated against Jews in Europe by European Christians. (But is there such a thing as collective trauma? Or is there really only the traumatized condition of several individuals represented down the generations as the experience of a unified nation?)[15] It is also perhaps rooted in a suppressed sense of guilt on the part of many liberal Israelis at the destruction of Palestinian society wrought by the establishment of a Jewish state, even if they justified this as historically necessary. After all, Walzer himself proposed that when liberals act immorally in the conduct of collective violence against enemies, this "leaves guilt behind, as a recognition of the enormity of what we have done and a commitment not to make our actions into an easy precedent for the future." What he does not say, of course, is that the guilt may be accompanied by deep resentment against those whom one has wronged.

At any rate, it is evident that Walzer does not examine the detailed interconnections between power and the emotions but the so-called rational principles by which present violence should be morally judged. He is right: most settlers are not murderers. But from a Palestinian perspective their existence as settlers isn't independent of the Israeli government's legal, administrative and military apparatuses, and that connection is what enables "the coercive transformation" of the Palestinian "way of life." I noted above that, according to Walzer, a fatal threat to political community, whether by ethnic cleansing or by "the coercive transformation of their way of life," could be the ground for engaging in otherwise morally unacceptable violence. Walzer, alas, fails to relate this ground for Palestinian militancy to his own argument.

In a review of the Spielberg film *Munich* published recently, Henry Siegman tries to do what Walzer fails to do. He argues that the bombings by Palestinian terrorists should be compared not with the retaliatory strikes by the IDF but with "how Israelis acted during their struggle for independence and statehood." Drawing on the archival researches of the Israeli historian Benny Morris,[16] Siegman cites the widespread massacres of Palestinian civilians perpetrated by the Irgun in the 1930s and by the IDF in 1948. "Of course," writes Siegman, "Israel's resort to ethnic cleansing and the massacre of civilians in its War of Independence does not confer any legitimacy on the morally indefensible atrocities committed by terrorists in the Palestinians' ongoing struggle for their independence," but—he goes on—it does expose the double standard of many commentators on the subject.[17] My reason for citing Siegman here is not polemical, however. It is not his call for even-handedness that interests me but his distinction between the violence integral to the founding of a political community and the violence used to defend and extend it—as in the military assaults by the IDF against Palestinians. I will pursue later the point that at a profound level the familiar separation between permissible and impermissible violence is more problematic than it appears at first sight.

So, war is a legally sanctioned concept, and the hateful killing perpetrated by unlicensed militants is not. And yet soldiers are taught to hate the enemy they are required to kill; the fact of killing being legally sanctioned is an abstract irrelevance. In this regard, soldiers are no different from terrorists. Of course, the latter are often militarily incompetent, not to say politically infantile, but that's not what is held against terrorism by state apologists, for the use of terror as such is not always inept: think of the firebombing of German and Japanese cities in World War II—in which hundreds of thousands of civilian men, women, and children were terrified and slaughtered—that accomplished exactly what it was designed to do.[18] What I want to stress is simply this: the sincerity of the terrorist's conscience, of the excuses he makes, is of no significance in the categorization of his action; the military commander's sincere conscience, on the other hand, may be crucial to the difference between an unfortunate necessity and a war crime.[19] That is why the unresolved argument about the World War II strikes against civilian targets tends to revolve around the question of its necessity—around whether without them more innocents would have perished in a war against an unjust and ruthless enemy.

So the word "terrorism" not only signifies culpability under state law but also, as Walzer's disquisition indicates, feelings of vulnerability: a terrorist is someone who creates a sense of fear and insecurity among a civilian population for political purposes. As such, the term and its cognates are certainly valid. My argument, however, is directed against thinking of terrorism simply as an illegal and immoral form of violence and advocates an examination of what the discourse of terror—and the perpetration of terror—does in the world of power.

Although war is a defined activity in international law, an activity that has a formal cause and a formal conclusion, this is clearly not to be confused with the beginning and end of organized killing by the state. The state's violence against civilians may precede and succeed war in the formal sense—especially in a war of independence (by whose unauthorized use of terror a sovereign state is founded) or in a "small war" (against so-called uncivilized populations, in which terror may be used precisely because they lack a sovereign state). Such violence is inseparable from the primary duty and the absolute right of the nation-state (or would-be nation-state) to defend, or achieve, or deny the claim of others to sovereignty. But as a specific *legal* category, "terrorism" is difficult to define because in doing so complicated *political* choices have to be made regarding the limits to established state authority and the rights of popular movements that challenge state authority. It was for this reason that the International Criminal Court rejected pressure by India, Turkey, and Sri Lanka to include terrorist acts as punishable offenses.[20]

In contrast, terrorism experts who are employed by the state, or would like to offer their services to it, propose that the definition of terrorism is an easy matter having nothing to do with politics. "Terrorism," writes one such expert, "is a generalized construct derived from our concepts of morality, law, and the rules of war, whereas actual terrorists are shaped by culture, ideology, and politics—specific inchoate factors and notions that motivate diverse actions."[21] In other words, the discourse of terrorism is dependent on a constructed object (*not* an imaginary object) about which information can be collected.

Every war requires the making of human killing machines, and the question of its legality tends to distract attention from this fact. "Basic training itself was often extremely brutal, even for conscripted recruits," writes Joanna Bourke.

> The most notorious training regimes were those conducted by the U.S. Marine Corps, but even in the other branches of the armed forces, violence was a common component of military training. In all these training programmes, the fundamental process was the same: individuals had to be broken down to be rebuilt into efficient fighting men. The basic tenets included depersonalization, uniforms, lack of privacy, forced social relationships, tight schedules, lack of sleep, disorientation followed by rites of reorganization according to military codes, arbitrary rules, and strict punishment. These methods of brutalization were similar to those carried out in regimes where men were taught to torture prisoners: the difference resided in the degree of violence involved, not its nature.[22]

The torture of prisoners is integral to the violence that the soldier in training learns. The *practice* of terror thus produces efficient soldiers and is an important part of the conduct of war, in the battlefield as well as in interrogation centers where vital information is obtained.

The *discourse* of terror enables a redefinition of the space of violence in which bold intervention and rearrangement of everyday relations can take place and be governed in relation to terror,[23] a space that presupposes new knowledges and practices. "Before the terrorist attacks of 9/11, there was no field called 'homeland security,'" writes Richard Falkenrath.

> Today, homeland security is a multibillion-dollar enterprise and the motivating force behind countless reforms across dozens of heretofore separate government activities. The need for this enterprise is not tied to the fate of al-Qaida or any other particular terrorist group; instead, it derives from the structural—and hence, for all intents and purposes, permanent—vulnerability of free and open societies to catastrophic terrorist attacks. This vulnerability existed before 9/11 and will continue to exist indefinitely. . . . Homeland security has no epistemic community to speak of, but needs one. Men and women from dozens of different disciplines—regional experts, terrorism analysts, law enforcement officials, intelligence officers, privacy specialists, diplomats, military officers, immigration specialists, customs inspectors, specific industry experts, regulatory lawyers, doctors and epidemiologists, research scientists, chemists, nuclear physicists, information technologists, emergency managers, firefighters, communications specialists, and politicians, to name a few—are currently involved in homeland security, but it is not enough merely to aggregate specialists. . . . Only a team of individuals with genuine crosscutting knowledge and experience will be able to understand the complexity of any particular homeland security challenge, devise an efficient and viable strategy for dealing with the problem, and implement this strategy effectively.[24]

The new epistemic community being called for is necessary to name and deal with what is claimed to be a new object in the world of liberal democracy—terror. Most of the activities of those already involved in countering terror may appear quite familiar: mass surveillance, individualized interrogation, transporting suspects to domestic and foreign torture centers, targeted assassinations, and military invasions on the grounds of preemptive self-defense. And yet the fact that a new epistemological object can be constructed through a war on terror is something new.

It is important to my argument that these actions not be seen as simple abuses of the executive branch, partly because the judiciary and the legislature can cooperate actively with the latter to uphold the rule of law in an overarching national endeavor and also because the constitutional scope of executive powers is subject to legal interpretation and political contestation.[25] In proposing that the space of violence enables the state in its triple aspect to extend its presence, I do not want to oppose the state to a passive civil society. It is not only the executive branch that occupies this space. All constitutional states rest on a space of violence that they call legitimate. In a liberal democracy, all citizens and the government that represents them are bound together by mutual obligations, and the actions of the duly elected government are the actions of all its citizens. When the government acts against suspected terrorists and inferior military opponents, everyone is (rightly or wrongly) involved in the space of violence. There may be criticism by particular citizens of the government's actions on moral or legal grounds, but until these are conceded constitutionally by the government, all citizens remain bound to the space of violence that its representative government inhabits.

Terror is also integral to modern subjectivities that fear not only the disruption of orderly life but also and especially the end of democratic institutions under the assault of barbarians, whether immigrants or terrorists.

Acts of war are not disturbing to most civilians when the human damage perpetrated by their armies occurs abroad. The Allied invasion of Nazi Germany in World War II was applauded by civilians at home. Terrorist acts, on the other hand, create anxiety because they occur at home. Talk of terrorism and the need to defend oneself against it can have a similar effect. When terrorists are seen as people engaged in conspiracies, one is induced to look for signs that point to something hidden (their motives are unexpressed).[26] How might these be found? Alternatively, how can one do a proper reading of signs to discover the threats posed by secret motives? In the United States, the Patriot Act, passed to deal with terrorists, provides the practical framework for undertaking such readings. According to many critics, the Patriot Act is an attack on constitutional rights.[27] But this kind of complaint rarely attends to the working of power/knowledge in the modern state. The project of "Defending America" calls for techniques aimed at discovering the objects that threaten.[28] The interrogation center is not merely a source of information and a place where abuse may happen. It is the site where a particular kind of identity is typified and dealt with and where the secrets of a danger are laid bare in the war against terror, which is a permanent state.

It has been widely reported that viewing the famous images of the towers under attack on September 11 was traumatic for Americans and that Americans have been understandably anxious ever since. Anxiety regarding the real motives of people (especially anxiety in Euro-America about Middle Easterners who are in process of assimilating Western culture) rests on the polysemy of signs. Roland Barthes once claimed that "traumatic images are bound up with an uncertainty (an anxiety) concerning the meaning of objects or attitudes. Hence in every society various techniques are developed [that are] intended to *fix* the floating chain of signifieds in such a way as to counter the terror of uncertain signs."[29] But Barthes did not note that authority seeks sometimes to eliminate uncertainty in signs, at other times to create it. Had he done so, he might have acknowledged that uncertain signs do not in themselves cause anxiety or terror—it is suspicion about their meaning that may do so. To take people in familiar situations innocently is to live without suspicion. It is to read people literally, to take their behavior as unproblematic, as harmless. To do a literal reading of texts (of what people say and do in their ordinary life) is not, of course, to repudiate figurative language; it is to be so familiar with the relevant grammar that one is unconcerned with the need to fix meaning. On the other hand, to ask suspiciously about the real meaning of the verbal and behavioral signs displayed by people one knows is to enter into the world of symbolic interpretation. And while hermeneutics doesn't necessarily spring from hostile suspicion, it always presupposes that what appears on the surface is not the truth and seeks to control what lies beneath. Through interpretation, it converts absences into signs.

A form of official hermeneutics—an official suspicion about meaning—has flourished in the United States since September 11 as part of the war against terror: namely, the interrogation of captured Muslims by U.S. officials. Here fear, uncertainty, and the ambiguity of signs are part of the space of violence to which I referred above. More than that, they are its precondition, for they allow state power to penetrate the density of ordinary life.

Much has been written about the fact that terrorism feeds off the disclosure of torture or cruel, inhumane, or degrading treatment in U.S. detention centers, that torture is illegal, immoral, and inefficient. Less attention has been paid to the role the idea of torture plays in the distinction between war and terrorism. For decades, the CIA has produced and distributed interrogation manuals in Latin America to personnel involved in counterinsurgency. Take, for example, the *Human Resource Exploitation Training Manual—1983*.[30] In response to criticisms of abuse, it carefully distinguished noncoercive from coercive methods. It now warns against using the latter and then describes the former in detail. The manual's overall concern is to teach interrogators ways in which the subject's "internal motivational strength" can be "exhausted" so that he/she is made to yield the necessary information.[31] "Inwardness" is assumed, cultivated, and targeted.[32] One has to know the subject's type well enough to read the signs that are useful for the regulation of organized violence—one's own and that of the enemy. One begins with a human body having an appropriate appearance and origin: racial, sexual, and religious categories are what give the interrogator his starting signs. But he has to go beyond the words spoken by the subject to other signs—mode of speech, gesture, posture, etc.—that indicate hidden meanings. How should the interrogator draw out these meanings given the constraints of humanitarian law?

The humanitarian discourse that denounces unnecessary suffering rests on assumptions both of what is unnecessary and of what constitutes *suffering*. In effect, it invites interrogators to devise techniques in which the suffering of detained subjects is necessary—that is, techniques for getting prisoners to yield actionable information efficiently. "Efficiency" is always contextual, and it presupposes attention to detail: Should the techniques here be mental or physical? How intense or light should they be? What if they leave body marks or lead to trauma—does either matter, and, if so, to whom? These uncertainties parallel those that the military commander in the field of battle faces and in relation to which he must make his strategic judgments. The prisoner's necessary suffering (which may be glossed as "not really cruel treatment") is directed at crippling his motivational strength. Techniques in the conduct of the war against terror—whether in the interrogation center or in the field of battle—require the redefinition of "necessary violence." Despite humanitarian principles that forbid torture, however, the use of painful methods remains important. Whether the systematic torture of captives is always inefficient is a topic of considerable debate in the liberal media, but what it certainly does do is produce two categories of human being: torturables and nontorturables.

These paired notions first appeared in Graham Greene's novel *Our Man in Havana* (1958), set in prerevolutionary Cuba. In a dialogue between Segura, the local chief of police, and Wormold, a British Secret Service agent, the former refers casually to certain persons not belonging to the "torturable class." Who does? asks Wormold. "The poor in my own country, in any Latin American country," replies Segura.

> The poor of Central Europe and the Orient. Of course in your welfare states you have no poor, so you are untorturable. In Cuba the police can deal as harshly as they like with emigres from Latin America and the Baltic States, but not with visitors from your country or Scandinavia. It is an instinctive matter on both sides. Catholics are more torturable than Protestants, just as they are more criminal... One reason why the West hates the great Communist states is that they don't recognize class-distinctions. Sometimes they torture the wrong people. So too of course did Hitler and shocked the world. Nobody cares what goes on in our prisons, or the prisons of Lisbon or Caracas, but Hitler was too promiscuous. It was rather as though in your country a chauffeur had slept with a peeress.

That, interrupts Wormwold, doesn't shock us any longer. To which Segura responds: "It is a great danger for everyone when what is shocking changes."[33] It is precisely such a shift in what is shocking, when the U.S administration readily resorts to torture in contravention of the Geneva Convention and human rights law, that seems evident today. But one should note that the torture of prisoners in Guantánamo, Afghanistan, and Iraq (as well as the outsourcing of torture to the Egyptian, Syrian, and Pakistani regimes) affects torturables only. More remarkable than the use of torture by a U.S. regime that is said to be undermining the rule of law in several respects is the absence of any sustained public outrage in the democratic societies of the West. The liberal sensibility is more discriminating in this matter than one may have thought. In a war against barbarians, the use of cruelty has always been more acceptable than it has been against civilized enemy populations. And, even today, there is no general sense of horror (as I elaborate that term in my final chapter) at the numerous atrocities committed or condoned by democratic governments. So perhaps there hasn't been a shift after all in popular Western notions of what is shocking.

The sensitivity to humanist criticism that is directed at interrogation procedures is also found in the conduct of war. The modern Western army is concerned with engaging efficiently with dangerous, because underdeveloped, peoples, in ways that are at once ruthless and humane, in which brutal attack may become a civilizing sign. Nineteenth-century Europeans typically saw the world divided into civilized and uncivilized nations, in which the former should stand as a moral light for the latter. But this worked the other way, too: it was held that the behavior of civilized nations should not fall to the level of the uncivilized. Hence Gustave Moynier, one of the founders of the Red Cross, could speak explicitly about the organization's "evangelical morality" in its effort to "civilize" European warfare. But this idea of achieving humane standards logically required a contrast: "Compassion," he wrote, "is unknown among savage tribes that practice cannibalism. . . . It is said that even their language doesn't have the words to express the idea, so alien is it to them. Savage peoples . . . make [war] to excess and give in without a thought to their brutal instincts, whereas civilized nations, seeking to humanize it, even admit that everything that happens is not [morally] allowable."[34] Civilized nations, being refined in manners and restrained by morality and law, are quite unlike the uncivilized. They should not fight as savages do, in brutal and terrorizing ways.

But the savage was not merely an abstraction for purposes of logical contrast; he was someone toward whom one could and should behave appropriately in war. Writing in 1927, U.S. Army captain Elbridge Colby noted: "The real essence of the matter is that devastation and annihilation is the principal method of warfare that savage tribes know. Excessive humanitarian ideas should not prevent harshness against those who use harsh methods, for in being over-kind to one's enemies, a commander is simply being unkind to his own people."[35] Captain Colby belongs to a dominant line of thinking and practice in Western colonial warfare. To him as to others, it is self-evident that since uncivilized opponents do not abide by international law, they cannot be protected by it; today, of course, this is said about those seen as, or suspected of being, terrorists.[36]

For many today, this seems to be vindicated by the claim that "terrorism has become bloodier," as it perpetrates "large-scale indiscriminate violence."[37] At the same time, it is claimed that in this war against an uncivilized opponent, the use of increasingly sophisticated information technology has allowed the military to identify its targets more accurately and thus to minimize collateral damage. What is certain is that by fighting the enemy at a distance, it has been able to minimize its own casualties. Unchallengeable air supremacy and precision weaponry make virtual impunity of the pilot possible. Furthermore, domestic public opinion in liberal democracies is critical of excessive war casualties in its armies. This humanitarian concern means that soldiers need no longer go to war expecting to die but only to kill. In itself, this destabilizes the conventional understanding of war as an activity in which human dying and killing are exchanged. The psychological effect of this unequal killing is mitigated by the fact that there is a long-standing tradition of fighting against militarily and ethnically inferior peoples in which it is proper that the latter die in much larger numbers. Since they do not value human life as the civilized do, they will expose themselves to greater risks, even undertake suicidal operations, and therefore suffer more casualties.

In fact, little attention has been paid in the growing literature on new military technologies and strategies to the continuities of the new wars with earlier colonial wars that were often called "small wars." In them, Euro-American soldiers discovered that the opportunities for killing were much greater than the risks of dying in battle and that "uncivilized" enemies were not entitled to be treated with the same restraint as "civilized" ones. A notable exception to the contemporary literature on new wars is Max Boot's *The Savage Wars of Peace*,[38] which argues that "small wars" have been—and still are—essential to the spread of freedom, progress, and peace. Therefore, insofar as military interventions by Western powers continue this colonial tradition, it should be evident that their primary aim is not the protection of life as such but the construction and encouragement of specific kinds of human subjects and the outlawing of all others.[39]

Despite the civilizing project of many new wars, their conduct produces contradictory results. Thus, in deference to humanitarian law, the military of a liberal state—unlike the terrorist—does not normally target civilians, *unless it is compelled to do so*, but overriding concern for its own military casualties (again, partly in response to humanitarian sensitivities) means it must choose a strategy in which more enemy civilians die. So, too, in the matter of dual-use targets. Because of military necessity, the military must inevitably target facilities such as electrical power plants that are crucial to the enemy's military but also to its civilians. The destruction of electricity-generating centers cripples water purification plants, hospitals, and so on, causing widespread death and disease among the civilian population. One interesting consequence of this contradiction (the killing of noncombatants that results from the new doctrine of striving for zero military losses as well as from bombing dual-use targets) is that motive becomes crucial to the distinction between collateral damage and war crimes.[40]

The just modern soldier incurs guilt when he kills innocent people; the terrorist does not. Or so modern theorists of just war tell us. Thus, in a recent article defending the Israeli invasion first of Gaza and then of Lebanon, Walzer writes: "When Palestinian militants launch rocket attacks from civilian areas, they are themselves responsible—and no one else is—for the civilian deaths caused by Israeli counterfire."[41] The political theologian Oliver O'Donovan has explained why state armies are morally superior by making a distinction between what he calls terrorism and insurgency in terms of motive: "The terrorist makes his point by slaughtering the inno-cent intentionally; the insurgent makes his by forcing his opponent to slaughter the innocent unintentionally."[42] This is precisely Walz-er's point. Zbigniew Brzezinski, however, has recently commented on this matter by reference to the most recent Israeli invasion of Lebanon: "I hate to say this but I will say it. I think what the Israelis are doing today for example in Lebanon is in effect—maybe not in intent—the killing of hostages. Because when you kill 300 people, 400 people, who have nothing to do with the provocations Hezbol-lah staged, but you do it in effect deliberately by being indifferent to the scale of the collateral damage, you're killing hostages in the hope of intimidating those that you want to intimidate."[43] Walzer, however, insists that there may be good reasons ("prudential as well as moral") for this kind of intimidation: "Reducing the quality of life in Gaza, where it is already low, is intended to put pressure on who-ever is politically responsible for the inhabitants of Gaza—and then these responsible people, it is hoped, will take action against the shadowy forces attacking Israel. The same logic has been applied in Lebanon, where the forces are not so shadowy."[44] Punishing civil-ians may be the only way to obtain results—given, of course, that an appropriate sense of guilt accompanies the action, because unlike barbarians civilized nations know what compassion is.

The moral advantage O'Donovan and Walzer give state armies over insurgents is evident. If the motive of military commanders is complex (they kill noncombatants but wouldn't if they didn't have to), however, couldn't the same be said of the terrorist whose killing of civilians is at once deliberate and yet coerced? He has reached the limit; he has no other option left—or so he claims, when he argues that in order to try to prevent "the coercive transformation of [his people's] way of life," he must carry out immoral killings. If he kills enough civilians (so he reasons), perhaps those who are politically responsible will respond in the desired way.

So: it is not cruelty that matters in the distinction between ter-rorists and armies at war, still less the threat each poses to entire ways of life, but their civilizational status. What is really at stake is not a clash of civilizations (a conflict between two incompatible sets of values) but the fight of civilization against the uncivilized. In that fight, all civilized rules may be set aside. Captain Colby observes of war with savage enemies: "If a few 'non-combatants' . . . are killed, the loss of life is probably far less than might have been sustained in prolonged operations of a more polite character. *The inhuman act thus becomes actually humane, for it shortens the conflict and prevents the shedding of more excessive quantities of blood.*"[45]

Clearly, Colby thinks the savage is incapable of such acts of humanity, and he is probably right. But what is especially intriguing is the ingenuity of liberal discourse in rendering inhuman acts humane. This is certainly something that savage discourse cannot achieve.

SUICIDE TERRORISM

I ARGUED IN the previous chapter that the categories "war" and "terrorism" are constituted according to different logical criteria, the one taking its primary sense from the question of legality and the other from feelings of vulnerability and fear of social disorder, and that they are not therefore mutually exclusive. It is not correct to say, as Walzer does, that "the peculiar evil of terrorism [is] not only the killing of innocent people but also the intrusion of fear into everyday life, the violation of private purposes, the insecurity of public spaces, the endless coerciveness of precaution" because war, whether just or unjust, does that, too. I also suggested that the brutality of a state army and of a terrorist group have much in common, that although in a formal sense state armies are subject to humanitarian law, this does not constitute as much of an obstacle to deliberate cruelty as might appear at first sight. To the extent that it is an obstacle to such behavior *as a matter of law*, this applies to independent individuals who act violently against states or to members of states that are too weak to afford them protection. Strong states protect their own and convict others as violators of humanitarian law of force. In this chapter, I want to discuss suicide operations through some current explanations that seek to distinguish them from acts of war. How different are they from each other?

One might think that one undeniable difference consists in destroying oneself in order to kill civilians one regards as one's enemies, and that this above all requires a special explanation. *Why did he do this terrible thing?* Terrible not simply because he killed innocents or was prepared to die (that's common enough in war) or simply because he killed himself (that's not uncommon in peace) but because he killed himself in order to kill innocents. Trying to pin down motives is difficult, however: When and how did the intention of undertaking a suicide mission come to be formed? Which desire predominated—killing oneself or killing others? What exactly did the suicide think the moment before he triggered the explosive: "I'm going to kill these bastards: they killed my brother," or "God will reward me for dying in His cause." or simply "I can't bear to live on under this cruel occupation"? Or was it perhaps something utterly different? Were unconscious desires hidden by his conscious language? Was he ecstatic? Or did he have second thoughts, doubts, regrets, as he proceeded toward his objective? If so, in what way and to what extent were they overcome? How does one set about answering such questions if the perpetrator is no longer alive? I do not say that such questions are always unanswerable but that the matter is far more complicated than is commonly supposed.

Is there a crucial difference between someone who kills in order to die and someone who dies in order to kill? Thus the sociologist Jean Baechler cites the case of the murderer Buffet who wrote to the French president before his execution demanding the "grace" of the guillotine: "To kill in order to commit suicide, that's my morality!" Baechler also cites examples of the reverse, the most famous being the kamikaze pilots in World War II who died in order to kill.[1] Such categorizations tend to draw on psychological models according to which suicide ("the solution to an existential problem")[2] can be regarded either as an instance of individual psychopathology or as a case of collective ideology. In both cases, there is a resort to causal as opposed to purposive explanation. What examples like Baechler's show, however, is that the end of an action is not defined merely by its ending: the end of suicide is killing oneself; the end of suicide bombing is killing oneself and others at the same time. The open-endedness of motive inevitably leaves considerable scope for interpretation.

Suicide attacks are therefore, above all, histories. In recounting plausible histories, they also employ fiction. Take the Columbia University professor of social science Jon Elster. Deferring to the authority of "a widely respected expert on this topic, Ariel Merari," Elster writes: "The mental state that actually triggers the act of detonating the bomb may therefore be ephemeral and something of an artifact rather than a stable feature of the person. When asked [by the U.S. Congress, before which he testified] how well he thought he understood the state of mind of suicide attackers in the minutes before he [sic] died, Merari answered: 'Some of them were elated, apparently. Ecstatic in the last moments' (CBS News, 25 May 2003)."[3] But how can one possibly know what went on in the mind of a surprise suicide attacker in the moment before she died? An interesting story about suicide depends, however, on assumptions about interesting internal states, and the mythology of suicide as pathology encourages fantasies of accessibility.

Explanations of suicide fighters tend to focus on the origin of motivation. It is not the effect of the bombing (which is plain for anyone to see) that preoccupies most Western commentators but the bomber's reason for doing what he or she does. That reason is often—not always—seen as being in some way pathological. Or as being alienated—that is, as not properly integrated into Western civilization.

But I think here of such unpredicted massacres as the one that occurred at Columbine High School when two heavily armed students killed and maimed a large number of their schoolmates and then shot themselves; the debate on what motivated them has been endless and (not surprisingly) remains indecisive.[4] A suicide bombing can be said to be more calculated than the school shootings: the combatant appears to be at once more in control of himself (he is disciplined in what he does) and less so (ruthless men have trained him). Yet these are conditions, not motives. The reason the combatant kills others by dying is often traced to the systematic deprivation and humiliation he has suffered—to his sense that, in confronting an overwhelming and ruthless adversary, common destruction is the only possible response (an expression of despair and rage?)— or to deep personal unhappiness. It is also ascribed to Islamic discourse because of his recorded proclamation before the operation, which typically uses a religious vocabulary—thus the highly ritualized proclamation is taken to correspond to his real motives. The motive and the action to which it leads are together regarded by most Western commentators as perverse because the agents have chosen death. But death here is an effect not a motive. "Intention," as I use the term, occurs at a causal level; "motives" do not. Motives are therefore often indeterminate. Why and when do people search for them? How do they recount the motives of suicide bombers? What signs do they take as visible indicators of invisible truth? And of what truth?

In the following discussion of some typical explanations of the suicide bomber, I suggest that they tell us more about liberal assumptions of religious subjectivities and political violence than they do about what is ostensibly being explained.

The well-known theorist of religious studies Ivan Strenski makes the point that explaining suicide operations in terms of "personal psychological motivation" isn't enough and urges that one needs a sociological and theological perspective. Drawing on the writings of the Durkheimian school, he proposes that the phenomenon is better understood through the religious concepts of sacrifice and gift than through theories seeking to explain suicide. Strenski reminds us that Halbwachs was perhaps the first theorist to distinguish analytically between suicide and sacrifice in his development and modification of Durkheim's thesis on suicide. For Halbwachs, the distinction turns on *society's* attitude, something most clearly evident in its ritual form. When self-immolation is expressed in a ritual form, it is to be read as sacrifice; without that form, it is suicide. "Sacrifice is a profoundly *social* action," Strenski echoes Halbwachs, "essentially involving a network of relationships, typically . . . actualized in terms of systems of social exchange. Sacrifice is not something to be understood solely in terms of the dynamics of an individual's psyche. What is more, sacrifice is not just a social deed. It also has potent religious resonance. . . . It is also a 'making holy,' as the Latin origins of the term indicate—*sacri-ficium*. Sacrifice for the Durkheimians is indeed a giving up, or a giving of, *that makes something holy*."[5] The sacrifice of oneself in the case under discussion, says Strenski, is made as a gift to and for the nation that is thereby sanctified: all suicide bombers believe they are giving their lives for the Palestinian nation, to the *umma*. "Without minimizing the importance of the utilitarian jihadist conception of these bombings [as a militarily tactic], as well as their multivalence," writes Strenski, "some of the many strands of meaning can be picked up that hang from the claim that these so-called suicide or martyrdom bombings need also to be considered carefully as sacrificial gifts [to Palestine]."[6] Strenski's analysis thus proceeds from the claim that since sacrifice is the essence of religious subjectivity, violence is integral to it.

Three comments are in order here, however. First, for Durkheim, virtually all acts are social, including suicide. Durkheim would almost certainly have included suicide bombing in his category of "altruistic suicide." Indeed, Durkheim was the first theorist to problematize the notion of "the individual" through an identification of the social determinants of that most personal of acts: suicide. In Strenski's account, we are still in the realm of looking for motives, of asking "what impels them to do it?" only now the motive is called "ritual," a theme that easily allows us to speak of the religious.

My second comment is that, in the Islamic tradition, sacrifice involving the slaughter of an animal (*dhabīha*) is made in response to a divine command (e.g., on the annual pilgrimage), or as thanks to the deity (e.g., on returning safely from a journey or recovering from a serious illness), or as a sign of repentance (called *kaffāra*) for particular transgressions. None of these criteria apply to the suicide bomber.

Third: Strenski's use of the idea of "making something holy" through sacrifice is less clear than it appears. I have written elsewhere about the problematic character of the concept of "the sacred," but, in the Islamic tradition at least, sacrifice does not make the recipient (God), or for that matter the sacrifiant (the person in whose name the sacrifice is made) or the victim, "holy." The rite itself—the words and movements necessary to it—might be glossed as "sacred," and it is true that the moral status of the sacrifiant is altered by the act of sacrifice, but that does not make him or her sacred. Strenski seems to have taken the Christian concept of Christ's supreme gift of himself as the model for sacrifice in general. But the Arabic for "gift," *hadiyya*, is never used to describe sacrifice, and *qurbān*—an Arabic word for sacrifice that is treated as central in Strenski's analysis—is more commonly used by Arabic-speaking Christians for Communion than by Arabic-speaking Muslims for animal sacrifice. In fact, the Qur'an uses the word *qurban* three times: at 3:183 to refer to burnt offerings according to Mosaic rites (there are no burnt offerings in Islam), at 5:27 to refer to the biblical story of Cain and Abel, and at 46.28 to refer to pre-Islamic beliefs about ritual mediation (the Qur'an rejects such mediation).

I will say more on the difference of the classical Islamic concept of martyr (*shahīd*) from the concept of sacrifice (*dahīyya*), but here I stress that if we pay closer attention to the way the concept of *shahīd* is deployed in historical as well as contemporary usage, we will see that its connection with sacrifice is contingent and that it doesn't fit with Strenski's use of that term. If one is to talk about religious subjectivities, one must work through the concepts the people concerned actually use.

A difficulty I have with Strenski's approach is that it is a forensic reading of motive. Its explanatory concern, like that of others, is with identifying culpability that can be established through the re-construction of a particular type of motive: According to this account, Palestinian suicide bombers are not sick, they do not perform their terrible acts because they are driven by an insupportable environ-ment. The suicide bombers are fully responsible—answerable—for their acts because they *choose* to justify their violence in terms of a discursive religious tradition, in which they choose to offer individual lives (their own and the lives of others) in exchange for a transcen-dent value. It is the free intention of the perpetrator that leads to the criminal act and not (as is often alleged) brutal subjection to Israeli occupation. That, at any rate, is how this kind of reading is made. By finding the culprit as well as the religious sources that feed his criminality, a danger to Israeli society is identified with precision; the state's extension of the space of violence in the cause of security is seen to be necessary. Thus although for the law it is the unlicensed act of killing civilians that defines the crime, for journalists and se-curity experts it is his motive for doing this terrible thing that is of primary interest. And yet, because the actor dies in the event, his motives are not fully retrievable. Ironically, it is only at the trial of someone who has failed to complete the operation that the motive of suicide bombers can be adduced. So the social scientist, novelist, and filmmaker endow the dead terrorist with the motives of the living. Strenski's redescription of motive in terms of the concept of sacrifice offers a religious model by means of which suicide bombing can be identified as "religious terrorism." And that appellation defines the bomber as morally underdeveloped—and therefore premodern—when compared with peoples whose civilized status is partly indi-cated by their secular politics and their private religion and whose violence is therefore in principle disciplined, reasonable, and just.

———

But one can do the reading in other ways, define and separate types of violent acts and the subjectivities to which they are attached, differently. Much will then depend on the overriding hermeneutic principle one adopts to reconcile apparent inconsistencies in the reading required by the explanation one favors. The result may not be incontestably better, but it can be more complicated than the one Strenski offers.

In a recent unpublished article,[7] May Jayyusi insists that suicide fighters must be understood in relation to new forms of political subjectivity that have been formed in the context of resistance to the particular powers that circumscribe them. To describe these powers (the Israeli military, the Jewish settlements, the Palestine Authority, and Islamic Jihad and Hamas), she draws on Carl Schmitt's idea of "the state of exception" via Giorgio Agamben's *Homo sacer* and stresses the importance of a developing political-ideological field—including Israeli policies of occupation and settlement, the Palestinian resistance, and international developments (the Iranian revolution) and agreements (the Oslo Accords). This is a larger story than the one told by Strenski, and it doesn't begin by trying to explain a *religious* act.

Oslo, Jayyusi writes, was an attempt to institute a local authority over the Palestinian population, charged with containing and subjecting it to a variety of exceptional regulations. In effect, the result of Oslo was that an entire occupied population was held hostage to the policing performance of the Palestine Authority. As the overarching state power, Israel was at once beyond the Palestinian zones and yet sovereign over them. (The ambiguity of where its unstated borders lie—what is inside Israel and what is outside—have long been part of its strategic advantage.) This means, Jayyusi points out, that the Palestine Authority was caught in an irresolvable contradiction: on the one hand, seeking national sovereignty and, on the other, conceding it indefinitely to the occupying power by agreeing unconditionally to carry out its policing function. Nevertheless, Jayyusi claims that something new did emerge with Oslo for the general population, something she calls "an imaginary of freedom."

It seems that at first the Palestinian population as a whole received Oslo favorably despite the misgivings of many. Thus, according to the polls, support for the militant Islamist movements dropped to about 13 percent when first the agreement was signed. But as it became clear that the secular political elites in the Author- ity were unable to develop an adequate politics in the contradictory conditions established by Oslo, popular support for the Islamists rose to about a third. But, of course, more was involved here than a response to public opinion polls. There was also the welfare func- tion of the Islamists, in which care and assistance were provided to all on a neighborhood basis and regardless of party affiliation. Furthermore, the mosque became the site of an Islamic discourse in which subjectivity was increasingly individuated, moralized, and linked to the movement as its collective representative.

Incompetent and corrupt, the Palestine Authority came to be gen- erally seen as lacking legitimate leadership and incapable of stand- ing up to Israeli power that had seemed in Oslo to recognize the possibility of a Palestinian state and that now easily denied it. The expansion of Jewish settlements in the West Bank and Gaza contin- ued, control of the water supply was withheld from the Authority, the pattern of new roads responded to the needs of the settlers and not to those of Palestinians. More land was confiscated by the state, more houses destroyed, militants as well as their kin punished. Add to all that the daily humiliation of all Palestinians at the many army checkpoints. Insupportable rage, says Jayyusi, was the con- sequence—and she cites Hannah Arendt's statement at this point ("rage arises 'only when there is reason to suspect that conditions could be changed and are not'"), relating it to the national struggle after Oslo. I suggest, however, that the relevance of Arendt's state- ment is not its reference to uncontrollable anger (planned suicide bombing is not an instance of uncontrollable rage) but its concern with an act of death dealing that reacts to injustice by transgress- ing the law. The stress here should be not on violence as such but on spontaneous action when legal political means are blocked. Be- cause, for Arendt, we may recall, the possibility of acting politically is part of what makes men individual and therefore human. It is also what offers them a secular form of immortality.[8]

The second uprising started in October 2000 after Ariel Sharon's provocative entry into the holy shrine of al-Aqsa to demonstrate Israeli sovereignty over it. This gave Hamas its opportunity to demonstrate its political initiative. On January 1, 2001, it launched the first suicide operation. Subsequently, suicide operations began to be undertaken by the other—secular—political factions and eventually by members of the population at large. It was Fathi Shikaki, founder of Islamic Jihad, who had launched, in the early eighties, what many Palestinians call the second round of armed resistance against Israel.

So there is an important Islamic dimension in the suicide operations, according to this story, but it is placed in a wider context than the one appealed to by Strenski and others. Islamic militancy is characterized by the fusion of two elements: the centrality of martyrdom (inspired by the Iranian example) and the individuating process (initiated and promoted by Hamas) centered on the mosque.[9]

Jayyusi's conclusion is a neat inversion of Agamben: "If 'homo sacer' is he who can be killed and not sacrificed," she writes, "then the martyr here inverses this relation to sovereignty, transforming himself into he who can be sacrificed but not killed. Many testaments of martyrs are signed with the words 'the living martyr,' ash-shaheed al-hayy. They can be sacrificed but cannot be killed, the koranic verse 'Do not count those who are martyred for the sake of God dead but alive with their lord' is the signature of every bayan."[10] So Jayyusi, too, draws on the religious idea of sacrifice, as well as on Palestinian politics, in her explanation of the suicide fighters' motives. But she includes an expressive element: the martyr demonstrates something by his violent death. The explanation itself is an optimistic one in which the Palestinian snatches the responsibility for his own life and death from the Israeli occupiers. This is arresting, but Jayyusi's explanation in terms of *shahāda* needs to be complicated further.

Actually, Palestinians, when employing a religious vocabulary, call all their civilians who die in the conflict with Israel *shuhadā* (plural of *shahīd*)—including innocents killed in Israeli operations against militants and stone-throwing boys shot by the Israeli army. Strenski's claim that *shahāda* (glossed as "martyrdom") is essentially connected to the ritual of sacrifice—that it is a form of sacrifice—cannot account for this wider category of *shuhadā*. What matters according to this latter usage is neither personal motive nor political expression but the fatal effect of a violent encounter with the occupying enemy. The violent death of *all* Palestinians in confrontation with Israelis, so one might suggest, is regarded as a sign that they have died as witnesses (*shuhadā*) to their faith—although there is no ritualized form to most of these deaths. As such, the *shahīd*'s death constitutes a triumph rather than a sacrifice.[11]

This usage fits with older conceptions of a death that needs special explaining. For over the centuries the Islamic tradition has described several ways of dying as *shahāda* that are not connected with war:

> To the Prophet is ascribed the saying that not only those who are slain for the faith are to be regarded as martyrs. Seven other causes of death are enumerated which make the sufferers worthy of the honorable title of a *shahīd*, and these are mainly calamitous or pathological causes, which have nothing to do with voluntary self-sacrifice for a great cause. In later times other causes have been added to these seven. He who dies in defense of his possessions, or far from his home in a strange country; he who meets his death in falling from a high mountain; he who is torn to pieces by wild beasts, and many more, are to be counted in the category of *shuhadā*.[12]

Thus to be struck by a fatal calamity, whether natural or human, is to be constituted as a sign of human finitude in the world created by an eternal deity. I therefore suggest that the reason Palestinian civilians who are destroyed under the Occupation are regarded as *shuhadā* is twofold: first, they have been struck by a catastrophe, and, second, their mode of death gives them immortality. The idea of immortality here is not strictly speaking physical because everyone recognizes that the individual's physical existence is ended by death. At any rate, to be struck dead by an external force has nothing to do with motives. But it does have to do with violence—violence not as it appears in the spectacular act of killing others by killing oneself (whether this can properly be accounted *istishād* is a matter of dispute among Muslim scholars) but as it relates to the idea of mortality. All untimely death that is not the result of legitimate punishment is a violation. The believer who dies in a so-called justified war (actively *or passively*) belongs to that category, but the category itself is not defined by participation in "justified war."

So one problem I have with Jayyusi's account is that in its emphasis on sacrifice it concedes too much to current fashions in explaining suicide operations as a perverse form of national politics and permits unhelpful references to a unique "culture of death." This doesn't mean that such a term is unusable but that it is used too crudely for the simple purpose of designating an illiberal perspective. Liberalism, too, I shall argue later, has its own culture of death.

But can one nevertheless regard suicide bombing as an expression of the political culture—the culture of death—that has emerged in modern times in the Middle East? Some commentators who have addressed this point do think so.

Bruno Étienne, a well-known French political scientist who specializes in North Africa, has tried to place suicide operators in the context of a long history of violence: precolonial repression (the Ottomans and then the modern Turks, as he points out, were scarcely gentle toward those of their coreligionists whom they dominated); colonial wars of conquest (in which ears and testicles were triumphantly collected by the French); colonial violence (of which Frantz Fanon wrote); wars of decolonization (in which both sides used torture, assassination, and systematic mutilation); the brutality of dictatorial regimes (whether nationalist or Islamist); the violence, finally, since the creation of the state of Israel, inflicted by the Israeli army on the Palestinian people at whose expense the state was established.[13] It is not clear whether Étienne is suggesting that the cumulative effect of historical violence in the Arab world *caused* the outburst of suicide bombing or whether he views such bombing simply as a continuation of the history of Middle Eastern violence. In either case, he takes it for granted that suicide bombing requires special theoretical attention.[14] Psychoanalysis might combine the two in the idea of sacrifice, which it explains as an unconscious desire for parricide. For Freud, it will be recalled, totemic sacrifice is the unconscious repetition of a primeval crime;[15] for others, like Money-Kyrle, the unconscious desire for parricide, acquired by each individual in his own development, is bound to the idea of gift.[16] My argument throughout has been that to take suicide bombing as sacrifice is to load it with a significance that is derived from a Christian and post-Christian tradition. Although in my view this makes it inappropriate as an *explanation*, I shall later suggest that as an *idea* it is an important part of the political imaginary of modern nationalism.

In the case of Palestinian combatants, Étienne points out, the enemy's force is far more powerful, and add to that the contempt they sense in the verbal charity of their Arab brothers, as well as the Israeli contempt symbolized by the wall and the many checkpoints. "These things have manufactured contempt and hatred, transformed hatred for the self into hatred for the Other. Absolute."[17] But where in all this is the mechanism of a hatred for the self to be located?

What is especially striking is how the widespread belief about tendencies inherent in monotheism allows Étienne to assimilate Islamic discourses on the subject to a Christian one—as Strenski does.[18] Yet compared with medieval Christian literature, there are actually very few medieval Islamic texts that deal exclusively with what is called in European literature "martyrdom." In any case, the concepts are not the same even if the words used (*martyr* and *shahīd*) are etymologically connected. I have already referred to the range of meanings for *shahīd*, including unintentional death, that sets it apart from Christian understandings of "martyr." The Qur'an, incidentally—and perhaps significantly—doesn't make explicit use of the word *shahīd* to signify someone who dies in God's cause. The verse most often cited in support of it (9:52) speaks of *husnayayn*, "the two best things," a phrase conventionally interpreted as "either victory or death in God's cause."[19] The concept of *istishhād* as a technique of *jihād* in which the combatant (*mujāhid*) annihilates himself is an entirely modern idea.[20]

Étienne's attraction to psychoanalysis is more interesting, however, even if his formulation of the Freudian idea of the death wish is not: "The death wish results from an overflowing of energies set free by the failure of the capacities to make representations: when there is no longer anything, no political model, no utopia, no hope, no solution—when the representations of the possible are frustrated, one explodes! This overflowing of excitation brings about a rupture: the actor, or the agent, as Pierre Bourdieu would say, is emptied of his own desires. He is then the object of a movement of disconnection for which the neurosis of war is the outlet."[21] Étienne's suggestion that the suicide fighter wishes to die because she lacks political imagination is not only implausible (consider the evidence that Jayyusi's account provides), it also rests on the assumption—which I will examine at the conclusion of this chapter—that politics and violence are mutually exclusive.

According to Freud, the pressure to prolong life and the pressure toward death are both permanent, contradictory drives in all living organisms. One need not agree with every shift in Freud's argument (or subscribe to Freudianism) to see that this idea raises questions about every individual's approach—now deliberate, now unconscious; now willing, now reluctant—toward her end. There is in Freud's account no simple way in which a death decided by the individual for himself can be explained. One may say that the suicide fighter is *driven* to annihilate herself in the enemy or that she *chooses* to destroy her enemies that way. But how to account for the difference between laying hands on oneself and making war? For

Freud, both are aggressive instincts, and the death instinct (like the instinct to extend life) is a transcendent power beyond the conscious subject while being at the same time his own desire. The playing out of this instinct—of the ability and willingness to wage devastating wars—appears most impressively among the so-called civilized nations, in spite of Freud's claim that the disciplining mechanism of guilt serves more and more to internalize aggression as civilization progresses. But guilt, I argued in my first chapter, is no bar to the repetition of transgression. And, contrary to Étienne (and Freud), war is not a neurosis but a collectively organized, legitimized, and moralized game of destruction that is played much more savagely by the civilized than the uncivilized. Nor is it suicide in any but a metaphorical sense. In fact, there is consistent evidence to the effect that rates of suicide tend to decline significantly in wartime.[22]

Étienne goes on: "But at what moment does an actor—whether manipulated or not—go on to the act of self-destruction? And in what 'objective' conditions does an entire society become 'mad' to the point of massacring its own children, as was the case in Algeria in the 1990s? . . . Self-hatred was going to be transformed into hate for the Other. All the more so in that Algeria, like most Arab countries, had lost its Other: the native Jew and the foreign (and foreign-tongued) European. Brother was thus alone face to face with his different brother, Kabyle, Berber, Arab, Islamist. This then produced a civil war that was to cause more than a hundred thousand deaths."[23] Here we seem to have an answer to the question I asked earlier about where the mechanism of self-hatred resides: according to Étienne, self-hatred is generated within and by the conduct of a vicious civil war, and the self is the nation in process of murdering itself. A complicated history of civil war is in danger of being reduced to a metaphor of suicide and equated with the real suicide of Palestinian militants—and then both are presented as expressions of an Islamic culture of death.[24]

Robert Pape, a political scientist, collects figures. He insists that statistics show suicide bombers must be understood as employing a
strategy of war.

I have spent a year compiling a database of every suicide bombing
and attack around the globe from 1980 to 2001—188 in all. It includes
any attack in which at least one terrorist killed himself or herself
while attempting to kill others, although I excluded attacks authorized by a national government, such as those by North Korea against
the South. The data show that there is little connection between suicide terrorism and Islamic fundamentalism, or any religion for that
matter. In fact, the leading instigator of suicide attacks is the Tamil Tigers in Sri Lanka, a Marxist-Leninist group whose members are from
Hindu families but who are adamantly opposed to religion (they have
committed 75 of the 188 incidents). Rather, what nearly all suicide
terrorist campaigns have in common is a specific secular and strategic goal: to compel liberal democracies to withdraw military forces
from territory that the terrorists consider to be their homeland. Religion is rarely the root cause, although it is often used as a tool by
terrorist organizations in recruiting and in other efforts in service of
the broader strategic objective.

Pape points out that these attacks are not random incidents but
part of organized campaigns and that in terms of casualties they are
the most efficient form of terrorism: Thus although only 3 percent
of all terrorist incidents consisted of suicide attacks, they caused
about half of all the fatalities, even excluding the large number who
died on September 11.[25] To signal to the citizens of liberal democracies that they face an intolerable cost is to compel their armies to
withdraw. Because they are widely mediatized, says Pape, terrorist
incidents "make a statement." One should add, however, that per-
formatives are a feature not only of terrorist incidents but also of
contemporary small wars (the 1991 and 2003 U.S. attacks against
Iraq are famous examples of political theater)—and indeed of all
popular politics that employ and respond to media images.

Pape is right to suggest that these incidents must be set in the context of what are in effect miniwars of rebellion. But he does not mention something about the states attacked that I think is more important than their liberal democratic status: their powerful armies. The insurgents are faced with an adversary that possesses formidable military weaponry as well as methods of controlling civilian populations in occupied territory that are often very effective, and this superiority cannot be met directly. Contrary to Pape's claim about the effectiveness of suicide bombings, however, Palestinian operations have in fact been counterproductive: militarily insignificant, they have strengthened public support in Israel for continued occupation, legitimated the Israeli government's strategies for further land expropriation, and evoked much Western sympathy for its war against terror.

Jayyusi, whom I have already cited, insists that

> the SB operations must be seen as acts that are performed as part of a continuum of resistance that has a history. According to IDF statistics the attacks that actually targeted the '48 territory represent only 4% of the total number of attacks, of which only a minority are SB operations. In comparing different testaments and checking it against the data, it clearly emerges that, within the discourse of Hamas and the practitioners themselves, there is not a strict demarcation between those who actually use their body as human bombs and those who go out to attack either settlements or army patrols with the intention of not coming back alive. Both are Istishhadiyyun, martyrdom-seekers where martyrdom itself is seen as the highest value.[26]

Unfortunately, Jayyusi, writing in 2004, doesn't say what period these statistics relate to, but the two claims she makes are worth pondering: (1) that the overwhelming majority of attacks against Israelis have been directed against West Bank settlers and the Israeli army and (2) that of these most have not been suicide bombings. If that is the case, then is the enormous attention given to the phenomenon of suicide bombings in Palestine and its roots in an Islamic culture of death simply a discursive construct of the Western media? In part perhaps, but not entirely—for reasons I will give in my final chapter.

While Pape's statistical data are intended to make the case that suicide bombers are motivated by strategic concerns, however, this does not satisfy everyone because it does not respond to the question that preoccupies so many: why do individuals agree to be recruited? The question presupposes the desire for an explanation in terms of motive—with the assumption that there must be a single clear answer to the question of motivation. Explanations in terms of religious (and especially Islamic) motive are still favored, partly because they provide a model that combines psychological elements (familiar from criminal trials) and cultural signs (distinguishing them from us), a model that lends itself to the discourse of the protection of civilization (committed to life) against barbarism (a love of death).

My final example is an article on contemporary *jihād* and martyrdom, in which Roxanne Euben explores some ideas of Arendt. While most commentators on the subject have tended to give either a political or a religious explanation of suicide terrorism, Euben avoids posing terrorism as the primary object of discourse and instead traces connections and tensions among public action, immortality, violence, and death in any political community. "I want to argue," she writes, "that, properly contextualized, *jihād* is a particularly illuminating way to investigate the implications of mortality and death for politics[,] . . . that in the hands of contemporary Islamic 'fundamentalists' (or 'Islamists'), *jihād* is neither simply a blind and bloody-minded scrabble for temporal power nor solely a door through which to pass into the hereafter. Rather, it is a form of political action in which, to use Hannah Arendt's language, the pursuit of immortality is inextricably linked to a profoundly this-worldly endeavor—the founding or recreating of a just community on earth."[27] Euben discusses the writings of Mawdudi and Qutb, two modern theorists of *jihād* for

whom the concept of *jāhiliyya* is central. *Jāhiliyya* referred historically to the period of pagan beliefs and customs of pre-Islamic Ara-
bian society and has since acquired the sense of moral savagery (the
Arabic root *jahl* signifies "ignorance" and "uncouthness"). Hence, according to these two writers, the elimination of *jāhiliyya*—by force
where necessary—is essential to the establishment of an *umma*, the
just community of Muslims. It is this community that "immortalizes
human deeds" (as Arendt would put it) while realizing God's plan on
this earth. The immortality that those who engage in *jihād* seek is at
once secular (of this world) and religious (of the next).

Euben's essay, like Étienne's book, doesn't distinguish among the
very different situations—Egypt, Palestine, Afghanistan, Iraq, and so
on—in which *jihādis* have fought. It is not obvious that all *jihādis* have
the same idea of the *umma*—or even that they all think they must
establish the *umma* as opposed to defending in a particular time and
place one that already exists or demonstrating their supreme loyalty
to it. In fact, it is not clear how many of the al-Qaeda *jihādis* are motivated by idealism or *ressentiment*—or just plain love of fighting and
killing.[28] Nevertheless, Euben's discussion does have the great merit
of moving away from trying to explain suicide bombing in terms
of motivation—a religious sacrifice (Strenski), an escape from political oppression (Jayyusi), a death wish (Étienne)—and moving toward
more difficult, less moralistic questions regarding relations between
personal mortality and political action. Her analysis of *jihād* and
shahāda is neither an apologia nor an indictment but a discussion
of the violence of those who endorse it as "a form of political action that endows human struggle to remake a common world with
existential weight. . . . While the *mujāhidīn* may seek the ever-elusive
rewards of the afterlife, *jihād* against modern *jāhiliyya* entails the
political struggle to realize the *umma* in a particular historical moment; in turn, it is the continued existence of the earthly *umma* that
immortalizes their efforts. I have suggested," she continues, "that
this recalls Arendt's elegiac evocation of a time and a place where
'men entered the public realm because they wanted something of

their own or something they had in common with others to be more permanent than their earthly lives.'"²⁹

For Arendt, of course, this world disappeared with the fall of Rome and the rise of Christianity, and it cannot be resurrected. But she saw in the replacement of the pagan investment in a worldly and collective immortality by the Christian emphasis on individual salvation not only an obvious ideological change but also the end of a certain attitude to politics—of political life as the space of an earthly permanence that can compensate for human mortality. It is neither the religious beliefs nor the military techniques of the *mujāhidīn* that finally interest Euben but the stimulus their political action affords for a reflection, not often found in liberal theory, on connections linking human finitude, violent death, and political community.

Euben ends by observing that a wide range of liberal theorists who otherwise disagree with Arendt's view of politics have this assumption in common with her: that politics, however it is to be defined, cannot have anything to do with violence. And yet—Euben reminds us—Athens itself was founded in violence, and its political sphere maintained by the violent exclusions of slaves, women, and foreigners. And so were all liberal democratic states in the modern world—and especially the United States—founded in massive violence and exclusions. "Augustine saw in this mutual implication of violence, death, and politics an other-worldly imperative," writes Euben in her concluding sentence, "the suggestion here is that these Islamist understandings of *jihād* recall less Augustine's lament than Machiavelli's suggestion, not that all politics is violent but that the violence of a founding may be the precondition to all politics."³⁰ Thus the evil of a founding violence is at the same time the good that the foundation brings forth.

Euben's elaboration of Arendt's idea about the connection between individual mortality and politics as immortality is helpful. But it should be pointed out that violence, in constituting the political sphere to which Euben alludes, extends beyond the moment of the founding of liberal states—which after all is a unique event in the history of each state, uniquely free in its constitutive violence, but an event in the past, something that, while it may give many liberals a bad conscience, is felt to be redeemed by the progressive elimination of political exclusions. More difficult is the question of the role of mortal violence in the continuing maintenance of the good political life. For in liberal secular society, one that apparently abjures political metaphysics, the morally autonomous individual has the right to choose his own life, and the sovereign state has the right to use violence in defense of the conditions for the good life. The right to punish enemies at home and abroad is fundamental to law,[31] and state law gives the individual his/her identity as a modern citizen.

Richard Tuck, historian of early modern political thought, has argued persuasively that "there is a kind of violence within liberalism of the Lockean type, which goes back to its origins in the violent politics of the Renaissance, in which liberty and warfare (both civil war and international conflict) were bound together."[32] A conception of politics as the pursuit of war by other means—inverted by Clausewitz later in his famous aphorism—was born in that epoch, as the state gradually acquired exclusive power to wage war externally and to impose punishments internally. That violence, Tuck thinks, underlies liberal doctrine and practice today. It is not simply that the liberal state requires armies to defend itself and prisons to maintain order. It is rather that violence founds the law as it founds the political community. Violence is therefore embedded in the very concept of liberty that lies at the heart of liberal doctrine. That concept presupposes—so Tuck maintains—that the morally independent individual's natural right to violent self-defense is yielded to the state and that the state becomes the sole protector of individual liberties, abstracting the right to kill from domestic politics, denying to any agents other than states the right to kill at home and abroad.[33] The right to kill is the right to behave in violent ways toward other people—especially toward citizens of foreign states at war and toward the uncivilized, *whose very existence is a threat to civilized order*. In certain circumstances, killing others is necessary, so it seems, for the security it provides. The arguments about preemptive versus preventive war surrounding the U.S. invasion of Iraq are a consequence of this doctrine.[34] But while arguments go on interminably, decisive military action can be taken without its being held accountable under humanitarian law—so long as the military belongs to a strong enough power.

The political interests of liberal democratic states are not confined to their sovereign territory, especially when the welfare of populations depends on changing political, economic, and cultural relations in other parts of the world. Whether military engagements beyond sovereign territory are conducted for legitimate reasons or not, they have always constituted an integral part of the right to defend oneself and one's way of life. It is a truism that industrial capitalism since the nineteenth century has been increasingly destructive of forms of social life, that its markets have dislocated persons and things throughout the world, that the pollution of its factories and transport systems had disastrous effects on the natural environment and global climate that all humans inhabit. And yet industrial capitalism is the volatile condition in which Western liberties have been constructed, defended, and gifted to the world. The violent freedoms of industrial capitalism can be said to have constituted political life as the space of an earthly permanence that can compensate for the death of the past—at the cost of a fatal threat to the future. For the modern sovereign state has an absolute right to defend itself, a defense that may—as the International Court of Justice has held—legitimately involve the use of nuclear weapons.[35] Suicidal war with incalculable global consequences exists in the liberal world as a legitimate possibility.[36]

But there is another, less dramatic aspect of modern state violence to which I want to draw attention and that informs liberal politics. The mobilization of individuals within and by the sovereign democratic state and the care devoted to its population have been at the heart of the liberal conception of the good life. And a guarantee of that life is the citizen-soldier who is prepared to kill and die for it, yet whose health, longevity, and general physical well-being are objects of the democratic state's solicitude. Taken together, these well-known facts hint at something unique about the violence intrinsic to modern liberty. This has to do partly with advanced technologies for death dealing. The fact that modern warfare has given birth to numerous inventions is well known. These include improved techniques for destruction, of course, but also for the restoration of human life. Important developments in surgery, psychiatry, and psychology, as well as in nursing and hospital administration, are famously connected with the demands and consequence of modern war.

I quote at length from the military historian John Keegan:

Weapons have never been kind to human flesh, but the directing principle behind their design has usually not been that of maximizing the pain and damage they can cause. Before the invention of explosives, the limits of muscle power in itself constrained their hurtfulness; but even for some time thereafter moral inhibitions, fuelled by a sense of the unfairness of adding mechanical and chemical increments to man's power to hurt his brother, served to restrain deliberate barbarities of design. Some of these inhibitions—against the use of poison gas and explosive bullets—were codified and given international force by the Hague Convention of 1899; but the rise of "thing-killing" as opposed to man-killing weapons—heavy artillery is an example—which by their side-effects inflicted gross suffering and disfigurement, invalidated these restraints. As a result restraints were cast to the winds, and it is now a desired effect of many man-killing weapons that they inflict wounds *as terrible and terrifying as possible.* The claymore mine, for instance, is filled with metal cubes . . . , the cluster bomb with jagged metal fragments, in both cases because that shape of projectile tears and fractures more extensively than a smooth-bodied one. The HEAT and HESH rounds fired by anti-tank guns are designed to fill the interior of armoured vehicles with showers of metal splinters or streams of molten metal, so disabling the tank by disabling its crew.

And napalm, disliked for ethical reasons even by many tough minded soldiers, contains an ingredient which increases the adhesion of the burning petrol to human skin surfaces.[37] *Military surgeons, so successful over the past century in resuscitating wounded soldiers and repairing wounds of growing severity, have thus now to meet a challenge of wounding agents deliberately conceived to defeat their skills.*[38]

Keegan points to a double passion. It is as though advances in the surgeon's healing art, on the one hand, and the production of ever more ingenious ways of wounding and maiming, on the other, were locked in an endless game of mutual provocation, of death and of life, which rich and technically advanced liberal states can play with endless variation.

I return finally to Euben's point about the violence necessary to the founding of liberal political community. Violence, I argue, is not only a continuous feature of such a community. The absolute right to defend oneself by force becomes, in the context of industrial capitalism, the freedom to use violence globally: when social difference is seen as backwardness and backwardness as a source of danger to civilized society, self-defense calls for a project of reordering the world in which the rules of civilized warfare cannot be allowed to stand in the way. The political theorist Margaret Canovan has expressed this view by way of a memorable metaphor: "Liberalism is not a matter of clearing away a few accidental obstacles and allowing humanity to unfold its natural essence. It is more like making a garden in a jungle that is continually encroaching. . . . But it is precisely the element of truth in the gloomy pictures of society and politics drawn by critics of liberalism that makes the project of realizing liberal principles all the more urgent. The world is a dark place, which needs redemption by the light of a myth."[39] The violence at the heart of liberal political doctrine makes this clear: the right to self-defense eventually calls for a project of universal redemption. Another way of putting this is to say (although Canovan is not so explicit) that some humans have to be treated violently in order that humanity can be redeemed.

But there is something else. The right of liberal democratic states to defend themselves with nuclear weapons—and this seems to be accepted by the international community—is in effect an affirmation that suicidal war can be legitimate. This leads me to the thought that the suicide bomber belongs in an important sense to a modern Western tradition of armed conflict for the defense of a free political community: To save the nation (or to found its state) in confronting a dangerous enemy, it may be necessary to act without being bound by ordinary moral constraints. As Walzer writes: "A morally strong leader is someone who understands why it is wrong to kill the innocent and refuses to do so, refuses again and again, until the heavens are about to fall. And then he becomes a moral criminal (like Albert Camus's 'just assassin') who knows that he can't do what he has to do—and finally does."[40] In this reasoning, can the killing of innocents by taking one's own life be the final gesture of a morally strong leader?

So how unique is suicide bombing? If it is special—and I believe that in a sense it is—this is not because of the motives involved. Intentions may be validly deduced from actions in the sense that they define the primary shape of the action (the agent deliberately kills himself together with others, and that is what makes it a particular kind of action), but motives are to be distinguished from causes, because we speak of motives when we demand an explanation in terms of reasons: "Why did he do it?" Not everything that is done has a motive, by which I mean that we ask for an explanation in terms of motive only when we are suspicious of what the action means. We are not satisfied with "He did it because he wanted to kill others (whom he regards as his enemies) by killing himself." We ask: Why?—and assume that there is something bizarre about the action.

But motives themselves are rarely lucid, always invested with emotions, and their description can be contested. They may not be clear even to the actor. Most important, explanations in terms of motives depend on typologies of action that are conventionally recognized and to which individuation is central: for example, by the judicial system that determines (by using one or other psychological theory) guilt and innocence, or by theologies of salvation that trace the origin and consequence of sin, or by a secular theory of the unconscious that claims to make us understand our perplexed unhappinesses. The uniqueness of suicide bombing resides, I think, elsewhere. It resides, one might say, not in its essence but in its contingent circumstance.

HORROR AT SUICIDE TERRORISM

IN THIS FINAL CHAPTER, I want to move away from the preoccupation with the meaning of suicide bombing and with the question of what motivates the bombers to kill innocent civilians by dying—of why people choose death rather than life. I want to reframe the question. I want to ask: Why do people in the West react to verbal and visual representations of suicide bombing with professions of horror? Unimaginable cruelties perpetrated in secret or openly, by dictatorships and democracies, criminals and prison systems, racially oriented immigration policies and ethnic cleansing, torture and imperial wars are all evident in the world today. What leads liberal moralists to react to suicide bombings with such horror? Why are there so many articles, books, TV documentaries, and films on the topic?[1] Why are people—myself included—so fascinated and disturbed by it? In what follows, I offer a tentative answer by looking at some modern conceptions of killing and dying that have emerged out of the Judeo-Christian tradition.

In a review of two books on Palestinian suicide bombers, the British psychoanalyst Jacqueline Rose notes that suicide operations do not kill as many civilians as conventional warfare does, and yet people react to them with exceptional horror. "The horror," she writes, "would appear to be associated with the fact that the attacker also dies. Dropping cluster bombs from the air is not only less repugnant: it is somehow deemed, by Western leaders at least, to be morally superior. Why dying with your victim should be seen as a greater sin than saving yourself is unclear. Perhaps, then, the revulsion stems partly from the unbearable intimacy shared in their final moments by the suicide bomber and her or his victims. Suicide bombing is an act of passionate identification—you take the enemy with you in a deadly embrace."[2]

Rose is right to contrast reactions to the massive killing of civilians in World War II—the saturation bombing of Japanese and Germany cities—with Western reactions to suicide bombers. (How does one compare the suffering of those who survive in the two cases?) Her question about horror is important, but she doesn't quite answer it. "The horror would appear to be associated with the fact that the attacker dies," she observes acutely but then moves—too quickly—from the reaction of horror on the part of those who confront it as an image to a puzzlement about the perpetrator's moral status ("Why dying with your victim should be seen as a greater sin than saving yourself is unclear.") The latter shifts our attention again to the question of what motivates the suicide bomber to take his own life. Although Rose is a sophisticated commentator, her account leads the reader to lose sight of the matter of the observer's sense of horror.

So: Why the horror? Is it because death and dismemberment happen suddenly in the midst of ordinary life? Aerial bombing does give at least some warning (sirens, searchlights, the drone of airplanes, the distant explosions), however ineffective the immediate possibilities of shelter may be. (Hiroshima and Nagasaki, on the other hand, were atom-bombed without any warning and with no opportunity for civilian escape.) There is no warning—so it is often said—when the suicide bomber strikes her victims out of the routine of everyday living. There is something to this, but as an explanation it seems to me inadequate to account for the more muted reactions to the continuing death or maiming of adults and children by land mines in the third world. True, for the Western media, the sudden death of Europeans is more shocking than that of non-Europeans, and there are historical reasons for focusing on non-European militants who kill Europeans. Western reports of Tamil suicide bombers in Sri Lanka and even of the many suicide bombers in occupied Iraq attacking fellow Iraqis do not display the same horror—or evoke it in a Western audience. All of this may be true, but it still doesn't tell us why *horror* is expressed, when it *is* genuinely expressed, and what it consists in.

There is certainly something distinctive about a suicide attack, and part of it is this: The bomber appears as it were in disguise; he appears anonymously, like any member of the public going about his normal business. An object of great danger, he is unrecognized until it is too late. Signs taken innocently are other than they appear. There is also something else, however, something that Rose identifies but does not go on to address: "The horror would appear to be associated with the fact that the attacker dies." Why is that significant? Every death of human beings that is witnessed, every sudden death of someone spatially or socially near, may evoke violent emotions: anguish, fear, rage. What is special about suicide?

In the Abrahamic religions, suicide is intimately connected with sin because God denies the individual the right to terminate his own earthly identity. In the matter of his/her life, the individual creature has no sovereignty. Suicide is a sin because it is a unique act of freedom, a right that neither the religious authorities nor the nation-state allows. Today, the law requires that a prisoner condemned to death be prevented from committing suicide to escape execution; it is not death but authorized death that is called for. So, too, all other convicts in prison, all soldiers in battle, and the terminally ill cannot kill themselves, however good they think their reasons for doing so may be. The power over life and death can be held legitimately only by the one God, creator and destroyer, and so by his earthly delegates. But although individuals have no right to kill themselves, God (and the state) gives them the right to be punished and to atone.[3]

In antiquity, by contrast, suicide was neither a sin nor a crime, although it was typically the elites, to whom that freedom was a personal entitlement, who could legitimately take their own lives. Political authorities could offer suicide to members of the elite as a legal option to being judicially executed (Socrates is perhaps the most famous example). Nietzsche insisted that this suicide not only foreshadowed the Crucifixion but was also, like the latter, despicable because both were "undefiant deaths" (thought there is an important difference here to which I'll return: Socrates' death was a private suicide, carried out in the small company of friends;[4] the Crucifixion a public demonstration of punishment and redemption). Nevertheless, it is not the fact that the subject has chosen suicide that critics like Nietzsche object to but its manner and meaning. They are asserting the secular humanist principle that *fighting* against the demands of external power is a sign of nobility. There is nothing horrible, so they seem to say, in violent death itself, only in the motive that defines it.[5]

But first: What is horror? Horror is not a motive but a state of being. Unlike terror, outrage, or the spontaneous desire for vengeance, horror has no object. It is intransitive. I find Stanley Cavell helpful here. "Horror," he writes, "is the title I am giving to the perception of the precariousness of human identity, to the perception that it may be lost or invaded, that we may be, or may become, something other than we are, or take ourselves for; that our origins as human beings need accounting for, and are unaccountable."[6] Horror, Cavell observes, is quite different from fear; it is not the extreme form of fear that we call "terror." If fearlessness is a possible alternative to terror, there is no parallel alternative to horror. I want to stress that in this sense horror applies not only to the perception that *our own* identities are precarious but also those of other humans—and not only the identity of individual humans but also that of human ways of life. As understood here, horror is not essentially a genre—the horror film or novel—that articulates a plot: sudden discovery of evil, fear of disaster. Horror is a state of being that is *felt*. Horror explodes the imaginary, the space within which the flexible persona demonstrates to itself its identity.

Let me concretize the idea of horror by reference to published accounts of suicide operations. The accounts typically refer to the sudden shattering and mingling of physical objects and human bodies. Here is a long description of such an event in Jerusalem:

> With my back turned to the door as I sat at the counter of a pizza parlor waiting for my order, I didn't see a man try to enter with a backpack slung over his shoulder. The pack contained a bomb. When a suspicious guard turned him away, the man ran to the door of the coffeehouse 20 feet away and blew himself up as two guards rushed him, shouting, "Duck, everybody!" I saw a flash out of the corner of my eye and an instant later heard the crack of an explosion. I knew instantly a suicide bomber had struck. "Damn, they've hit Jerusalem," I thought as I ran toward the door. The eerie silence in the immediate aftermath was broken first by the sound of a woman's whimper blossoming into a full-blown scream. As I hit the five or six steps down to the street, a woman in shock swept past me with her arm extended, looking at her bloody hand as though it were a foreign object. The first thing I saw was the severed, bloody head of the suicide bomber, sitting upright in the middle of the street like a Halloween fright mask. The sight was confirmation of an ugly truth I had learned from Israeli police spokesman Gil Kleiman at the day's first bombing. "The weakest part of your body is your neck," Kleiman told me after a worker had climbed a 20-foot ladder to retrieve the bomber's head, which the blast had torn from his body. The acrid smell of dynamite and burned hair was in the air. In the coffeehouse, the walls were charred and the floor was littered with shattered furniture. There was no movement. A fluorescent light glowed behind the counter. "Stop looking around. Do something. Help," I told myself. Two feet away on the asphalt was a woman, her skin ghostly pale. Later, from newspaper photos, I learned the woman's name was Nava Applebaum. Her father was the emergency room director of a hospital and a specialist in treating

suicide bombing victims. He had met Nava there to have a father-daughter talk on the eve of her wedding. For her wedding, the 50-year-old Cleveland-born doctor had prepared a book with sayings from family members and himself, biblical passages and marital advice. Twisted bodies. Applebaum, 20, was curled on her side gasping for breath, her father's body eight feet away, his back and head smoldering. I wasn't sure what the force of the blast had done to her internal organs, but either the concussion of the blast or her collision with the pavement had twisted her left arm at the shoulder and elbow in a direction a limb is not intended to go. The heat of the blast had singed her hair gray. I huddled next to her and pressed my fingers against two dime-sized holes that shrapnel had torn in her neck. . . . As ambulances arrived and Israeli police and rescue workers responded, I yelled to catch their attention. One worker, then two, joined me. One felt for a pulse. His shoulders sagged. Nava was dead, along with six others. They placed her body on a gurney and rushed it away.[7]

The account I have just quoted reflects feelings of anger, distress, and compassion. But one gets a glimpse of something else, too, a sense of something distinct from sympathy for the suffering of victims and survivors or from outrage at the destruction of human life: the woman's bloody hand is described as an alien thing; the bomber's head in the street as a fright mask; a man's back and head burn like coal; his daughter's arm is not a natural limb. One is presented here not just with a scene of death and wounding but with a confounding of the body's shapes. It is as though the familiar, reassuring face of a friend had disintegrated before one's eyes. All this is interwoven with touching details (names and personal histories of some of the victims) based on information that could only have been acquired long after the event described so dramatically—by which I don't mean to imply that it is untrue but that it is a construction. The narrative is intended as a way of making readers *feel* the horror of a suicide bombing, to feel helpless in the face of a sudden attack against everyday life and, above all, the loss of that ordinariness in which human identity resides. There are two crucial things here: the writer's visceral sense of horror (which might have been felt witnessing a terrible accident) and his reconstruction of it specifically as the work of a suicide bomber.

In fact, horror is more often encountered in recitations of war, most acutely in retrospect by those who have experienced it. Theodore Nadelson, a psychiatrist who treated Vietnam veterans suffering from post-traumatic stress disorder, has written about their experiences of war, its terrors and enchantments. He has also written briefly (too briefly) of the aesthetics and pornography of killing,[8] the sense that many soldiers in war have of affirming life through the very destruction of other human beings (regardless of whether they are noncombatants), their erotic involvement with death (including their own), and the intoxication with killing that Marines call "eye-fucking."[9] I reproduce at length one of the many accounts given to him by anguished patients:

> I got a photograph. I'm holding two heads—standing there holding two heads by their hair. Can you believe it? Well, there were other guys walking around with heads on poles—like savages, like long ago . . . and nothing un-normal about it, that's the un-normal part—it was normal, real, it was accepted. They took a picture of me. That's how I remember it because of the photo. That's why I still have it—reminds me of those times—without the picture I won't believe it in peacetime. . . . In 'Nam you always got something to do, ambush, clean out a VC [Vietcong] tunnel . . . you do it so you can get out, get food, get water, and maybe, but you don't want to think of it, you [will] get back home, back to the "real world." But now you are in hell and you act it. You don't dare think of home, no way. If you try to get home, you worry about trying to save yourself, you get dead. So nothing matters. The VC I killed . . . Jesus! Well, you had to do it. You had to do it to get out of there. I didn't care about the VC—they would have killed me. But the women and kids? First I was picking them [children] up after the gunships shot up a ville. Then I capped them

too. They'd grow up to kill you—maybe that was the story. But that's crazy—but like I said crazy was normal there. Unless you accepted that as normal, you could not live through it. They would do things, then it's over, and you go on. Hell, they [the VC] would do it to you, you have to do it to them a hundred times harder and worse. . . . So these guys found these women in a village and they started to rape them. Yeh, and they are banging away, and then they take out their K-bars, for God's sake! And they are stabbing them, crazy, out of control, and banging away—crazy—and still doing it when the women are dead. You understand? Maybe you understand . . . but it isn't possible to get people to understand who were not there. It was terrible what I—we did—but we all did it, those good guys I knew. All good, do anything for you. I can say it, I loved them. . . . But the worst thing I can say about myself is that while I was there I was so alive. I loved it the way you can like an adrenaline high, the way you can love your friends, your tight buddies. So unreal and the realest thing that ever happened. Un-fucking-imaginable. And maybe the worst thing for me now is living in peacetime without a possibility of that high again. I hate what the high was about, but I loved the high.[10]

Nadelson's patients, all deliberately trained by the state to become determined killers, were not unusual as troubled veterans go—and neither were their reported experiences, their painful sense of confusion that the experiences gave rise to.[11] They not only try—with evident difficulty—to narrate what they have done to others (and themselves) in war, to articulate and separate entangled feelings of tenderness and cruelty; they are in the end unable to give a coherent account of themselves as human beings. The narrator is at once perpetrator and victim. The inability to recount that experience, to grasp it verbally, is essential to its horror. Dave Grossman writing of the "sea of horror that surrounds the soldier and assails his every sense" in battle, quotes from a World War II soldier's memoir: "You tripped over strings of viscera fifteen feet long, over bodies which had been cut in half at the waist. Legs and arms, and heads bearing only necks, lay fifty feet from the closest torsos. As night fell the beachhead reeked with the stench of burning flesh."[12] But in this narrative there is no specific perpetrator, only an attempt to depict the horrific experience of war. Horror itself requires no culprit, although it can be discursively fed into the nation-state's claim to find one through the law. (The law is nothing if it does not define culprits.)

In eighteenth-century Europe, aesthetic and religious reflection turned directly to the idea of horror. In *A Philosophical Enquiry into the Origin of Our Ideas of the Sublime and Beautiful* (1757), Edmund Burke argued that pain and pleasure were incompatible (such that more of one meant less of the other) but that pain always evoked greater passions than pleasure. Pleasure, however, was not to be confused with what he called "delight": precisely because the latter can be attached to pain and danger, it draws us in horrified fascination to catastrophes. The power that excites this mixture of delight and pain is Burke's "Sublime," a power that cannot be clearly defined (delimited). Hence infinite emptiness, darkness, and silence were inhuman, manifestations of a timeless absence of form—and therefore not only a source of fear of the unknown but also of awe experienced as horror. Burke does not mention the Crucifixion, but the catastrophic and brutal death it represents is at once an object of horror and of love—and thus sublime. (For Freud, the Sublime was a survival from the forgotten psychic condition of childhood in which the earliest horrors of an unformed self were encountered, but as a quasi-religious experience it was also to be understood as the return of the primitive in an apparently modern and secular context.)

There is, of course, a well-known theological response to the horror of formlessness that early modern Christians were more than familiar with: In the Bible, it is the power of the deity that gives form and identity to something without it ("And the earth was without form, and void; and darkness was upon the face of the deep").

According to Genesis, the creation of the world consisted in giving form and identifying each form by name ("And God called the dry *land* Earth; and the gathering together of the waters called he Seas: and God saw that it was good"). The culmination of this work, of course, is man—who named and thus identified every living creature—and then woman. Only the shaping, naming, and maintaining work of the deity keeps horror at bay for humans; that is one reason every step in the formation of the world, as represented in Genesis, is repeatedly pronounced "good." Yet the deity himself, to the extent that he is limitless and indescribable, remains a source of horror, the only power capable of destroying all form, of absorbing all identities. From horror, refuge may be taken in reverence.

The Bible is full of destructive as well as creative acts in which identities are undermined or claimed. The most famous example in the Old Testament of autodestruction that is also a creation is recorded in chapter 16 of Judges. Samson, scourge of the Philistines, is eventually taken captive by them through the treachery of his foreign wife, Delilah, depilated, and blinded.[13] But in prison his hair (and with it his strength) grows again, and in the temple of the idol Dagon, where the Philistines are gathered in large number, he carries out his terrible deed of ritual destruction. The Bible recounts this story—the killing of a large number of unsuspecting innocents, including the boy who had led Samson in his blindness—as an act of triumph. It is a religious suicide through which God's enemies are killed with God's assistance and a new political world is initiated. Samson's final act redeems not only his own heroic status but also his people's freedom. The Bible doesn't linger over his motives; instead, it describes the ceremonial nature of his burial and hints at a new collective beginning—at what we would now say is the making of history.

As a narrative of struggle, betrayal, and suffering, the Samson myth has lent itself to various modern projects, secular and religious. It has been used in numerous works—operas, poems, paintings, novels, and movies—in the history of Western art. Perhaps this is because the spectacular final act of suicide and destruction is art—or, at any rate, the aesthetic performance of an idea.[14] In the celebrated seventeenth-century poem *Samson Agonistes*, John Milton identified himself in his blind days with the captive hero and prophesied the ultimate victory of his side (faithful to the God of Abraham) over the royalist worshippers of the false god Dagon. The horror of a mass killing is translated into a story of redemption. But there is something more than an allegorical reading here. Frank Prince, poet and Milton scholar—and editor of the Oxford edition of *Samson*—speaks of the "beauty of moral severity" displayed by this great work: "Intransigence of judgement, firmness of faith, the acceptance of both action and suffering, are themselves moving and beautiful," he writes.[15] Whatever one may think of this critic's suggestion, it is evident that the aesthetic sensibility in Milton's *Samson* is multiple and not reducible to the singularity of mere pathology.

Interestingly, the story is also told as a national myth of *secular* redemption through the establishment of a Jewish state in Palestine. In 1927 the revisionist Zionist Ze'ev Jabotinsky rewrote it as a simple, romantic novel, in which motives are fleshed out and realist detail added. Even the Philistine guards (invented by Jabotinsky) are given a dignified end in the destruction of the temple. They are representatives of a nation who, with typical fatalism, must accept their own defeat in the face of a new power—a new truth—in the land.[16] Here, as in all recountings of the story, Samson is not the destroyer of identity but the creator of one that is heroic—although the heroism of Jabotinsky's nationalist tale is quite different from the one Milton depicted. Jabotinsky has no sense of the tragic, merely an eye for the exotic in the public theater of violence.

Today, in Israel, Jewish children are taught to revere Samson the hero as the archetypal "tough Jew." According to a recent book by the Israeli writer David Grossman, the story of Samson articulates the problematic quality of Israel's use of power. Grossman thinks that, like the biblical hero, Israel has not yet developed a proper awareness of its immense strength. Grossman explains this in psychoanalytic terms: in the case of Samson, via a speculative history of an emotionally deprived childhood; in the case of the Jews, with reference to a long history of victimization. The contemporary Jewish state, unaware of its own strength, tends to resort too quickly to force—and to use it excessively without being fully conscious of what it is doing. The myth of Samson, Grossman suggests, accounts for the mythic, uncontrolled quality of Israeli power; that power is reflected in and performed through a tragic story.[17]

Clearly, when aggressive suicide is read as the initiation and affirmation of collective identity, it does not invite an immediate response of helpless horror. Sometimes, however, the possibility of unimaginable horror is deliberately and publicly hinted at, as in the name Israel has chosen for its nuclear arsenal: "the Samson option." That option is the readiness to undertake a nuclear strike that, in a very narrow geographical space, will certainly result in the joint destruction of Israel together with its enemies. The horror that is deliberately displayed here as a chosen possibility is embedded in the state's narrative of virtue: of its duty to use *any* means to defend its way of life. But, of course, horror conveyed discursively is not horror directly experienced.

I turn now specifically to the dissolution of the human body and the horror this generates.

In *Purity and Danger*,[18] Mary Douglas famously argued that in every culture, whether primitive or modern, things are categorized according to distinctive criteria whose confusion is viewed as an outrage. When boundaries are breached—when form is endangered—they must be restored: rituals of avoidance, punishment, and purification are ways of doing just that. It is the absence of rituals for dealing with transgression, not the fact of "matter out of place," that generates horror.

Purity and Danger was a seminal anthropological work that inspired much scholarship in several disciplines on the subject of taboo. One wishes, however, that Douglas had had more to say about power, as an earlier anthropologist to whom she is indebted had done. In his posthumous book *Taboo*,[19] Franz Steiner pointed out that in its original Polynesian context the word indicated danger, and since the idea of danger is at once political and metaphysical (even the word "danger" once signified "being in the power of, under the dominion of"), it is linked to a range of practices by which attempts are made to protect valued identities, beliefs, and forms of life. Put another way, the anxiety that what is valued is being menaced can be dealt with by systematic distancing, expulsion, and punishment.

Steiner's tracing of a genealogy of the concept "taboo" (which had found its way from anthropology into psychoanalysis) problematizes the way in which the concept of "the sacred" was deployed in anthropological theology. At the same time, he also rejects Freud's assumption that primitives were like neurotics in confusing veneration with horror, the former being an attitude that was rationally justifiable and the latter not. The confusion, according to Freud, consisted in an inability to distinguish what was really dangerous to the self from what was merely imagined to be so. (Steiner could have pointed out, but does not, that the two are not equivalent: veneration is an action within a relationship; horror is a frozen state of being.) Against Freud's elision of the primitive and the infant, Steiner insisted that religion was concerned in different ways with powers that threatened or defended the integrity of being human. But it is particularly his discussion of the chiefly political organization in Polynesia—the context in which the word "taboo" was first identified by Europeans in the eighteenth century and then later generalized to a range of different phenomena—that opens up another avenue for understanding horror in relation to power's ability to impose limits (taboos) where these have been transgressed. These include the familiar religious sins of heresy, blasphemy, and sacrilege or, in a secular world dominated by the modern nation-state, the crimes of treason and terrorism. The horror that these acts may produce is the result of their deliberate transgression of boundaries that separate the human from the inhuman, the creature from the Creator. Horror is the total loss of practical and mental control.

Thus, while dominion—divine or worldly—is typically concerned to deal with the crossing of limits that variously constitute the human and to require restorative work when transgressions occur, it does not forbid the killing of human life itself. On the contrary, power dissolves living bodies as punishment for outrages committed or as sacrifice in "just" wars. But it also regulates the transformation of all dying bodies—the transition from life to death—by way of mortuary and mourning rites, cemeteries and war memorials. The body of the deceased is central to these rituals of transition from the world of the living to the world inhabited by the dead, and mourners may experience horror if the rituals of transition are ignored and profaned. Relatives of the deceased may experience considerable disquiet if the corpse is irretrievable in its entirety—whether this be the result of drowning at sea or to an explosion—so that it can be properly dealt with, honored, or appeased. That is one reason why the modern state ("representative of the nation") seeks to obtain the dead bodies of its soldiers both during and after hostilities. For those who believe in another world as well as those who don't, the indeterminate status of the recently dead is a source of great anxiety because death threatens the identity of the living to whom the deceased was bound. Proper words and gestures—even angry ones—are a means of responding appropriately to this threat. They serve—in the funerary rites and later—to incorporate death into the predictable continuity of a form of life and thereby to suppress the thought that it is life that is contingent.[20] Thus it is not the occurrence of death as such in which horror resides but the manner in which it occurs and how the dead body is dealt with by the living.

The transition from life to death by social reincorporation can also take the form of public punishment, including ritualized torture.

In *Les larmes d'Éros* (1961), Georges Bataille refers to a photograph—one of several—of a young Chinese man being subjected to the ritual punishment of "the hundred pieces," in which he is slowly cut up alive. The photograph was taken in 1905 and reproduced in 1923 by Georges Dumas in his *Traité de psychologie*. Bataille writes:

> I have been told that in order to prolong the torture, opium is administered to the condemned man. Dumas insists upon the ecstatic appearance of the victim's expression. There is, of course, something undeniable in his expression, no doubt due at least in part to the opium, which augments what is most anguishing about this photograph. Since 1925 I have owned one of these pictures. . . . I have never stopped being obsessed by this image of pain, at once ecstatic and intolerable. . . . What I suddenly saw, and what imprisoned me in anguish—but which at the same time delivered me from it—was the identity of these perfect contraries, divine ecstasy and its opposite, extreme horror.[21]

Part of the horror for Bataille seems to lie in the fact that the victim's face exhibits unbearable pain that is at the same time an expression of orgiastic abandon—the horror in this case is not, as he says here, the opposite of the latter but the union of the two.

Late medieval paintings on death, punishment, and atonement typically juxtapose youthful beauty with its ugly end: famously, they dwell on the inevitability of human decay, the fleeting (and often costly) character of pleasure. The punitive character of medieval Christian (and Muslim) morality has been much written about by moderns. And yet in secular modernity eroticism is sometimes deliberately linked to sadism—the sex instinct, Freud said, is always intertwined with the instinct of aggression. Of the paintings reproduced in *Les larmes d'Éros*, two might be seen as emblematic of this intertwining. First: Hans Baldung Grien's *Love and Death (Vanitas)* (1510) shows a nude young woman with long tresses absorbed by her image in a hand mirror and, hovering behind her with one arm raised above her head and the other clutching at her modesty scarf, a corpse whose decaying flesh barely conceals his skeletal frame— a classic representation of memento mori. The second picture is

André Masson's *Praying Mantis* (circa 1920), which depicts a naked woman lying—whether in ecstatic abandon or unbearable pain is not clear—with a man-sized praying mantis atop her with one limb in her crotch and his mandible kissing her face—or perhaps chewing at it. (Is this a misogynist allusion to the figure of the female praying mantis biting off the head of the male after copulation?)

There is a long Christian tradition of depicting—in words and images—the agonies endured by sinners after death. But these medieval works do not deal with horror in Cavell's sense; their purpose is to evoke extreme fear of divine punishment in the hearts of sinful believers. Masson's secular representation, on the other hand, makes no pretense at teaching a moral lesson. It simply illustrates in a disturbing way the Freudian proposition that the pleasure principle and the death wish—copulation and suicide, love and murder—are two faces of one natural reality. The sources of horror are already here, in the way we live and die, and not in a world to come.

I return to the torture of "the hundred cuts." What is represented in that photograph is not merely the dissolution of a living human body—and therefore of its identity. For Bataille, it also seems to be an intimation of something else: the possibility that the distinctions by which all recognizable, nameable human life is lived can be dissolved in ecstasy. Slowly, agonizingly, in exquisite delight—Burke's sense of "delight"—the living body of the condemned man becomes a mound of dead flesh.[22] In this transfiguration, the very possibility of ethics appears to be undermined. When no signs of the living body can be relied on, the ground that sustains the sense of being human—and therefore of what it is to be humane—collapses. What seems to horrify is the ease with which the boundary between what is alive and what is not—between the sanctity of a human corpse and the profanity of an animal carcass—can be crossed.

In 1949 Georges Franju made a documentary about a slaughterhouse in a Parisian suburb called *Blood of the Beasts* (*Le sang des bêtes*) that was to become a classic of surrealist cinema. The studied depiction of industrial death produces an effect of overwhelming horror in most audiences. Adam Lowenstein, in a fascinating monograph on horror films, draws on Walter Benjamin's idea of allegory to argue that "*Blood of the Beasts* insists on disclosing connections between everyday life and the horrors of history."[23] In particular, Lowenstein joins critics who have made the connection between the grim labor of the abattoir and the Holocaust. But I disagree here: the experience of horror (as opposed to the horror story) does not depend on interpretation, whether allegorical or symbolic. It does not convey meanings: *it is a state of being*. The scenes of unbearable pain, of blood-soaked death, of life transformed into meat—all depicted unemotionally in the film—require no allegorical reading, no sudden discovery of evil. They do not symbolize the murder of human beings. The routine killing of life is itself shocking, the treatment of living animals as industrial products grotesque. The mechanized killing in Nazi concentration camps was undoubtedly facilitated by treating victims as *untermenschen*, as animals, and that is certainly part of *its* horror. But the emotional effect of a documentary about an abattoir at work does not depend on its being read as a Nazi death camp. Horror, I want to insist, is essentially not a matter of *interpretation*.[24] When the viewer makes a connection between the abattoir and the death camp, she has gone some way to mastering horror and begun to develop an ethical judgment. What I want to say is not that horror is natural (indeed, it is always mediated by sediments and traces that have been inscribed in the body) but that it requires no discursive effort.

Recall the utterly horrific suicide in Michael Haneke's recent film *Caché*: a brutal act of self-destruction (he slits his own throat as in the ritualized slaughter of an animal) by a man who has never before shown any sign of violence or even any hatred for the person who has done him terrible wrong. The force of the shock resides not in anything *representational* but in the treatment of a human being as an animal that has to be killed appropriately when it is to be consumed. But the power of the image (which is *not* a representation of reality) is far greater than any story we invent for it. The protagonist, in whose presence the suicide occurs, is certainly horrified, but this doesn't open up for him any critical self-reflection. The point here is not, as an unsympathetic reviewer of the film in the *Nation* put it,[25] that the Arab conveniently kills himself in an act of symbolic self-negation in relation to a Frenchman. Rather, it is the horrible impact of that performance in itself that could (but doesn't as far as the protagonist is concerned) push viewers to reflect on the implications of suppressed memory—biographical as well as national—that constitutes, at least in part, what individual modern subjectivities are. By the end of the film, the protagonist is clearly in a state of shock, but he doesn't ask himself, "Why did he do this terrible thing? Was I in some measure responsible?" Instead, he takes a sleeping pill and asks his wife that he not be disturbed.

When Bataille writes, however, that he was horrified—and fascinated—by the photographic image, one needs to look at the faces of the onlookers and of the executer in the picture: they do not seem to express horror (any more than the workers in Franju's abattoir do), although they are looking not at an image but at the calculated act of violence itself. This suggests that since the actual witnesses to the ritualized punishment did not regard the scene as Bataille did, the gap between representation and perception is where human identity resides and that it is the tension between them that constitutes a permanent threat to it. The protagonist in *Caché* was probably horrified, but there is no evidence that he was able to move beyond that state into one of self-understanding.

Beyond this intersubjective horror at the destruction of the human body, one should perhaps mention another: the helplessness of an aging person regarding her own body, the body (perceived in reflection) in which her identity has been rooted. "When I read in print Simone de Beauvoir, it is a young woman they are telling me about, and who happens to be me," writes the author.

I thought one day when I was forty: "Deep in that looking glass, old age is watching and waiting for me; it's inevitable, one day she will get me." She's got me now. I often stop, flabbergasted, at the sight of this incredible thing that serves me as a face. . . . While I was able to look at my face without displeasure I gave it no thought, it could look after itself. The wheel eventually stops. I loathe my appearance now: the eyebrows slipping down toward the bags underneath, the excessive fullness of the cheeks, and that air of sadness around the mouth that wrinkles always bring. *Perhaps the people I pass in the street see merely a woman in her fifties who simply looks her age, no more, no less. But when I look, I see my face as it was, attacked by the pox of time for which there is no cure.*[26]

There is, I think, a sense of horror—as Cavell conceives it—that comes through in this passage, and not mere regret or disgust.

The significance of this process lies not in an awareness of approaching death or of weakening powers but in *the irresistible dissociation between self and body*, between, on the one hand, the stationary image of an embodied identity built up in one's full vigor and, on the other hand, a body less and less able to respond adequately to the routines and expectations attached to that self-image. Memory mocks the present. If memory is the reproduction of the past in the present, there is a parallel process in an aging body that reproduces the future in the present. Physical and mental decay are not merely anticipated intellectually but embodied in the present as extensions: failing eyesight, hearing, and strength; the loosening of skin and muscle; the distortion of body and rotting of flesh. Passion, attention, and memory are together attenuated: unassisted, life declines into nonlife. Whereas the past is lodged in uncertain memories and is thus increasingly uncertain, the future acquires an increasing physical reality. *Inscribed in the body is an image of the future that is nothing more than a continuous unbinding or emptying.*[27] Repressed horror typically attaches to that process.

Subjects can and sometimes do end the perceived threat of decay to their identity by committing suicide. (Note incidentally: suicide bombers are never old, which suggests that agility and physical confidence are more important to their performance than an appropriate motive.) That drastic solution, however, is also an end to identity itself, at least for the subject, though not for those who survive. For in modern society generally suicide tends to produce anguish among those who are rejected by that self-punishment and who are therefore compelled to bear within themselves the accusations of the dead. When these accusations are unaccountable, unrelatable to a remembered past, the anguish congeals as horror. In an important sense, every suicide causes close relatives and lovers who are left behind to die in some measure.

In the most famous suicide in Judeo-Christian history, however, a suicide that helps to define the tradition, the potentiality of horror is translated through a history of ethical interpretation and learnt sensibility into a productive complex.

In that history, God's only begotten son gave his life willingly and deliberately in order to redeem mankind: the supreme sacrifice.[28] Although he did not murder himself, he devised that he should be cruelly killed. The Crucifixion has long been a model in Christendom for legal punishment, so that a convicted victim's suffering has been seen as the repayment by which social and metaphysical order can be restored, as a means of cultivating absent virtue, as an example to others of the death that is at once sin and the cleansing of sin.[29] In fact, Christ's indirect suicide—his public torture—constitutes a paradox: it is at once a loving gift and a model of unjust suffering. There is an echo of this paradox in secular humanism: One must urge the citizen-soldier to give up his life so that a particular way of life may be reproduced—a *sacrifice*. And yet one may not permit the death penalty because as a legal *punishment* it may be undeserved and as inflicted *death* it is always irretrievable. Humanists—even secular humanists—are impressed by the possibilities of repentance and moral improvement. For them, the theological idea of redemption through repentance is a primary concern and often more important than the subjection of humans to cruelty.[30] As many reformers have argued, although repentance may not be a substitute for suffering, anguish is a sign that genuine repentance has occurred.

The Crucifixion is the divinely planned punishment of an innocent man, his vicarious suffering for humanity's sins. It carries a terrible gift: life everlasting purchased by a cruel death. The success of this supreme act of good is paradoxically dependent on a supremely (and convolutedly) evil act: the betrayal by Judas of his master, in which the latter colluded. The relevant passage in the *Gospels* makes this clear:

> When Jesus had thus said, he was troubled in spirit, and testified, and said, 'Verily, verily, I say unto you that one of you shall betray me.' Then the disciples looked one on another, doubting of whom he spoke. Now there was leaning on Jesus' bosom one of his disciples, whom Jesus loved. Simon Peter therefore beckoned to him, that he should ask who it should be of whom he spoke. He then lying on Jesus' breast saith unto him, 'Lord, who is it?' Jesus answered, 'He it is, to whom I shall give a sop, when I have dipped it.' And when he had dipped the sop, he gave it to Judas Iscariot, the son of Simon. And after the sop Satan entered into him. Then said Jesus unto him, 'That thou doest, do quickly.' Now no man at the table knew for what intent he spoke this unto him. For some of them thought, because Judas had the bag, that Jesus had said unto him, 'Buy those things that we have need of against the feast'; or, that he should give something to the poor. He having received the sop went immediately out: and it was night."[31]

What is striking in this well-known passage is that Satan is said to enter into Judas the moment he receives the order from Jesus to perform the act that will initiate the great drama of salvation, an expression of the paradox that the greatest gift to humanity must pass through the worst of evil.

But once we come to Christ's death, we are given to understand that its cruelty resides not simply in his physical suffering but in the fact that all human beings are ultimately responsible for it by reason of their sinful indifference. Thus cruelty consists not only in the intentional infliction of suffering on others but in a deliberate indifference to it. In the Crucifixion, however, the violent breaking of the body is not an occasion for horror (as in the Chinese torture of a hundred cuts); it becomes the source of a transcendent truth through a story, a fable. It also constitutes, in and through violence, the universal category of "the human" to whom the gift is offered (unlike Samson's suicide that reclaims the identity of a particular nation). In short, in Christian civilization, the gift of life for humanity is possible only through a suicidal death; redemption is dependent on cruelty or at least on the sin of disregarding human life.

If the Crucifixion represents the truth of violence, what is its significance in a secular age? In popular visual narratives (film, TV, etc.), the male hero often undergoes severe physical punishment or torture at the hands of ruthless men,[32] but his acute suffering is the very vindication of truth. The audience suffers with him and anticipates a healing. This replays a modern secular crucifixion story in which the truth of the lonely figure is sustained by his willingness to suffer in mind and in body, to undergo unbearable pain and ecstasy that can become through sympathy an exquisite part of the spectator's own sensibility.[33]

Modern liberal democracies are avowedly humanist and secularist, and liberals take their distance from the religious zealotry that wreaked havoc in Europe's early modernity. The medieval sensibilities that accompanied religious cruelties are regarded by them with professed horror. Yet the genealogy of modern humanist sensibility joins ruthlessness to compassion and proposes that brutal killing can be at once the vilest evil and the greatest good. "With surprising consistency, though to varying degrees over time and with shifting emphases," writes World War I historian Richard Gamble, "Americans have been habitually drawn to language that is redemptive, apocalyptic, and expansive. Americans have long experienced and articulated a sense of urgency, of hanging on the precipice of great change. . . . They have fallen easily into the Manichean habit of dividing the world into darkness and light, Evil and Good, past and future, Satan and Christ. They have seen themselves as a progressive, redemptive force, waging war in the ranks of Christ's army, or have imagined themselves even as Christ Himself, liberating those in bondage and healing the afflicted."[34] And more vividly, in the words of American orators themselves, here is a direct analogy between divine sacrifice and the United States' war casualties: "Christ gave his life upon the cross that mankind might gain the kingdom of heaven, while to-night we shall solemnly decree the sublimest sacrifice ever made by a nation for the salvation of humanity, the institution of world-wide liberty and freedom."[35]

Historians of Christendom have stressed the importance of late medieval thinking about atonement—particularly about Christ's final agony and its meaning for human redemption. They show how, through image, word, and deed, Christ's cruel death on the cross helped to create among pious Christians a distinctive sensitivity to human pain.[36] A sign of one's repentance was the measure to which one empathized with the *human* suffering of Christ—of Christ who was no longer (or not only) "the King" but also "the Man who restored man."[37]

In the fifteenth and sixteenth centuries, so-called Passion tracts, depicting in great detail Christ's pain and pathos, became very popular and were produced in several European languages.[38] The painting and words in which Christ was represented as the ultimate martyr and his life presented as the model for redemptive imitation (*Imitatio Christi*) became an essential part of the Modern Devotion, especially in its "stress on the personal relationship between Christ and each individual."[39] This passive merging with Christ's suffering gave way eventually to secular sensibilities that assumed a more active attitude to pain by refusing in all conscience that human suffering had any virtue whatever and elevating the virtue of compassion in relation to it. And yet, ironically, the idea of sacrificing individual life for the sake of national immortality in war as in peace has become quite familiar.[40] If "dying for the nation" sounds a little quaint and suspect to liberals today, "dying for democracy" seems to be more respectable.[41]

I want to suggest that the cult of sacrifice, blood, and death that secular liberals find so repellent in pre-liberal Christianity is a part of the genealogy of modern liberalism itself, in which violence and tenderness go together. This is encountered in many places in our modern culture, not least in what is generally taken to be "just" war. Take, for example, the moving volumes of war poetry written in the early part of the twentieth century: some critics have noted that the English poets of the Great War—Rupert Brooke, Siegfried Sassoon, Wilfred Owen, Robert Graves—were able "to express gentleness, tenderness, loving kindness, and love for each other" only when their readiness to kill was the accompaniment of these sentiments.[42]

Today, this contradiction is a part of a modern liberalism that has inherited and rephrased some of its basic values from medieval Christian tradition: on the one hand, there is the imperative to use any means necessary (including homicide and suicide) to defend the nation-state that constitutes one's worldly identity and defends one's health and security and, on the other, the obligation to revere all human life, to offer life in place of death to universal humanity; the first presupposes a capacity for ruthlessness, the second for kindness. The contradiction itself constitutes a particular kind of human subject whose functioning depends on the fact that the contradiction has to be continually worked through without ever being resolved.

"Dying to give life" is also found elsewhere in modern liberal culture. Anthropologists who have studied the medical practice of organ transplants write that the expression "giving life" is commonly used by organ procurement organizations.[43] This phrase must surely resonate, in a Western, humanist society, with Christ's gift of life to those who will receive it. But the use of this expression suppresses two horrifying elements in the whole business of organ transplants: first, there is the market for body parts, in which the transfer of life is dependent on the circulation of money; second, and connected with this, is the incitement to violence on the bodies of individuals ironically called "donors." This is not merely because there is a flourishing black market in organs secured in dubious circumstances from the healthy poor. It is also that certain kinds of transplant (liver, heart, lung, etc.) rely on a new mode of determining death—brain death—that allows the rapid removal of fresh organs. Sophisticated new technologies and arguments are thus at the center of what it means to die, to kill, to have an identity—at the center of the seeming paradox that new life can be obtained from a dead or terminated body, that one's identity depends on a body that is and yet is not entirely one's own.[44] State law in liberal democratic societies seeks to resolve these problems of life and death, but it is continually undermined by the way the modern culture of death feeds our modern passion for life—at least *our* life.

I argued earlier against the idea of a clash between so-called Judeo-Christian and Islamic civilizations. Others who have dismissed this thesis have begun to insist that the significant clash is within Muslim society, between modern liberals and fanatics. But it should be evident that there are disturbing contradictions in modernity, too. The contradiction between compassion and ruthlessness and its capacity to generate horror in the liberal mind is a distinctively Western one.

For most witnesses, horror—a compound of pain and delight or (as Bataille put it) of ecstasy and unbearable pain—is generated by the unexpected image of a broken body, a shattered human identity. There are few things as shocking as a sudden suicide in one's presence. A suicide operation, in which many die and are wounded, extends that shock. A possible refuge from horrified helplessness in that case is righteous anger directed at the perpetrator of the deadly violence.[45]

So what happens if the perpetrator of death dealing dies of his own free will at the very moment of his crime? What, in other words, if crime and punishment are united? Refuge from the helplessness of horror, as I said earlier, may be taken in enraged self-affirmation, in a rhetoric against death the dissolver of identity. It may also lead to the construal of horror as a crime—to the desire to punish the criminal, the separation of crime and punishment. Mortal vengeance separates by eventalizing, by countering death as loss with death as restoration, the former a brutal crime and the latter a just satisfaction. Durkheim's famous thesis on criminal law, it may be recalled, was that all legal punishment is based on a sense of popular outrage and is therefore motivated by passionate vengeance.[46]

Mortal vengeance is death for death, the democratic principle of the substitutability of individuals, in death as in life. Revenge always justifies itself as fighting back, which is why it requires that crime and punishment be separated in time. It is when this eventalization is impossible, as in suicide bombing, that a fundamental sense of identity—of witnesses who identify with the dead and depend on retributive justice to produce a sense of satisfaction—may be radically threatened and horror may seize them.

This returns me to the question with which I began: Why do Westerners express horror at suicide terrorism—what is so special about it? In trying to answer it, I offered several reasons, each of which points to identity being destroyed, a process felt more acutely by Europeans when they learn that Europeans have been killed by non-Europeans—because that is where they have learned to invest an aspect of their identity as humans. Let me spell these reasons out briefly. First, an unexpected suicide is always shocking, especially so when it also occurs in public and when it involves the shattering of other human bodies and their belongings, a sudden disruption of the patterns of everyday life, a violence in which death is unregulated by the nation-state. Warfare, of course, is an even greater violation of civilian "innocence," but representations have sedimented in us so as to see that *in principle* war is legitimate even when civilians are killed—that *in principle* deaths in war (however horrible) are necessary for the defense of our form of life. Here, the language of "civilization" and "barbarism" comes readily to hand rather than the more superficial "clash of civilizations." The second reason is that since crime and punishment, loss and restitution, are impossible to separate and since that separation is essential to the functioning of modern law on which liberal identities—and freedoms—depend, deaths in suicide operations are especially intolerable. Third, there are the tensions that hold modern subjectivity together: between individual self-assertion and collective obedience to the law, between reverence for human life and its legitimate destruction, between the promise of immortality through political community and the inexorability of decay and death in individual life. These tensions are necessary to the liberal democratic state, the sovereign representative of a social body, but they threaten to break down completely when a sudden suicide operation takes place publicly and when its politics is seen not to spell redemption but mutual disaster. Finally, I suggest the possibility that a highly emotional thought imposes itself on secular witnesses belonging to the Judeo-Christian tradition: the thought that the meaning of life is, as Kafka put it, death and only death. That catastrophic and brutal death can be, as the Crucifixion taught believing Christians, an occasion of love for *all* the dead. This is impossible on the occasion of a suicide bombing because there is no redemption there—none for the perpetrator, none for the victims, and none for those who witness or contemplate the event.

In the suicide bomber's act, perhaps what horrifies is not just dying and killing (or killing by dying) but the violent appearance of something that is normally disregarded in secular modernity: the limitless pursuit of freedom, the illusion of an uncoerced interiority that can withstand the force of institutional disciplines. Liberalism, of course, disapproves of the violent exercise of freedom outside the frame of law. But the law itself is founded by and continuously depends on coercive violence. If modern war seeks to found or to defend a free political community with its own law, can one say that suicide terrorism (like a suicidal nuclear strike) belongs in this sense to liberalism? The question may, I think, be more significant than our comforting attempts at distinguishing the good conscience of just warriors from the evil acts of terrorists.

EPILOGUE

I BEGAN THESE REFLECTIONS about suicide terrorism immediately after September 11, 2001. Since then, there have been four assaults by the United States and its allies against "Islamic terror," in two of which (Afghanistan and Iraq) the USA was the major warring party and in two (Gaza and Lebanon) the crucial political supporter and arms supplier of the major warring party (Israel). At the time of writing, all four wars are still ongoing and have already resulted in massive losses of life that immeasurably exceed anything terrorists have managed to do. This imbalance is not a matter of bad motives versus good but simply of greater technological capability. Western states (including Israel) have now massacred thousands of civilians and imprisoned large numbers without trial; they have abducted, tortured, and assassinated people they claim are militants and laid waste to entire countries. Their opponents, no doubt, would have done the same if they could. But this display of destruction leaves me with several worrying questions to which I have no adequate answers: (1) Is there something terrible about the mere fact of large numbers being killed, or is it the notion of disproportionality that disturbs? (2) If the civilized Western states did not intend the large numbers of civilian deaths in the wars they have initiated, does this

absolve their leaders of all culpability? (3) If the vast majority of the citizens of these democratic countries support the destructive policies of their elected governments, are they in some sense also its partial agents? I have read some of the debates on these matters without becoming any the wiser.

In the long perspective of human history, massacres are not new. But there is something special about the fact that the West, having set up international law, then finds reasons why it cannot be followed in particular circumstances. I find this more disturbing than the sordid violence of individual terrorists. It seems to me that there is no moral difference between the horror inflicted by state armies (especially if those armies belong to powerful states that are unaccountable to international law) and the horror inflicted by insurgents. In the case of powerful states, the cruelty is not random but part of the attempt to discipline unruly populations. Today, cruelty is an indispensable technique for maintaining a particular kind of international order, an order in which the lives of some peoples are less valuable than the lives of others and therefore their deaths less disturbing.

On BBC Radio 1 on Thursday, July 13, 2006, the well-known British actress Maureen Lipman was asked whether Israel's military response to the actions of Hamas and Hezbollah wasn't a little disproportionate. "What's proportion got to do with it?" she replied, "It's not about proportion is it? Human life is not cheap to the Israelis. And human life on the other side is quite cheap actually because they strap bombs to people and send them to blow themselves up."[1] What Lipman meant by speaking of human life was, of course, not *human* life but *Jewish* life. Indeed, it was not only that human life "on the other side"—that is, Arab life—was quite cheap but precisely because it was cheap that it could be so treated by the Israeli army. The perception that human life has differential exchange value in the marketplace of death when it comes to "civilized" and "uncivilized" peoples is not only quite common in liberal democratic countries; it is necessary to a hierarchical global order. It is quite true that the death of poor people in the world does not matter as much as the death of people in affluent societies. In saying this and acting on this belief, the patterns of living and dying in the world come to be affected by it.

All this is fairly familiar stuff, and yet our media and our political potboilers remain obsessed with the ruthlessness of jihadists and the dangers of an unreformed Islam. Some of those who focus on this theme are probably driven by cynical motives, but for many if not most the talk of an Islamic threat is closely connected to the horrifying image of the suicide bomber. In this book, I have tried to think about the reasons that make this image so compelling. I have come to the conclusion that some of these reasons are religious, but not religious in the sense that Western commentators take this to mean. For the latter, suicide bombing is seen as a violent expression either of a perverted, totalitarian Islam or of a primordial (and therefore irrational) religious urge that secularism has overcome. When I refer here to religious reasons, I have in mind the complex genealogy that connects contemporary sensibilities about organized collective killing and the value of humanity with the Christian culture of death and love, a genealogy that I think needs to be properly explored. For what needs to be identified here is not simply the willingness to die or to kill but what one makes of death—one's own and that of others.

The modern secular world retains a contradictory view of life and death, although that view is not a simple replay of Christian paradox. The genealogy I have referred to is not a line of patriarchal descent (A begat B who begat C); it is a shifting pattern of convergence and dispersal of contingent elements. The contradictions are many, and their consequences unpredictable: On the one hand, every individual must face his or her own mortality; on the other hand, the science of genetics promises an unending life. On the one hand, the sanctity of human life is valued above all things, while, on the other, there is the sanction to kill and to die, and to do whatever it takes, to defend a collective way of life. On the one hand, the life of every human has equal value; on the other, the massacre of civilized humans is more affecting than that of the uncivilized. Good arguments (and bad) are available to anyone who wants to justify the conduct of insurgents or of soldiers, of armies on the battlefield or of torturers in state detention centers. Because in our secular world all these forms of violent conduct are thought ultimately to secure a kind of collective immortality—what some scholars call civil religion and others pseudoreligion.

NOTES

1. Nearly five years after the terrorist attack on September 11, and three years after the devastating war in Iraq, public opinion in the United States remains remarkably hostile to American Muslims.

A new Gallup poll [posted August 10, 2006] finds that many Americans—what it calls "substantial minorities"—harbor "negative feelings or prejudices against people of the Muslim faith" in this country. Nearly one in four Americans, 22%, say they would not like to have a Muslim as a neighbor. While Americans tend to disagree with the notion that Muslims living in the United States are sympathetic to al-Qaeda, a significant 34% believe they do back al-Qaeda. And fewer than half—49%—believe U.S. Muslims are loyal to the United States. Almost four in ten, 39%, advocate that Muslims here should carry special I.D. That same number admit that they do hold some "prejudice" against Muslims. Forty-four percent say their religious views are too "extreme." In every case, Americans who actually know any Muslims are more sympathetic. The poll was taken at the end of July [2006] and surveyed 1,007 adult Americans.

(www.editorandpublisher.com/eandp/news/
article_display.jsp?vnu_content_id=1002984956)

2. For example, Alan Dershowitz, professor of law at Harvard, put the prosecution's case against Muslim suicide bombers: "Why do these overprivileged young people support this culture of death, while impoverished and oppressed Tibetans continue to celebrate life despite their occupation by China?" The answer was obviously religion—a certain kind of religion: "The time has come to address the root cause of suicide bombing: incitement by certain religious and political leaders who are creating a culture of death and exploiting the ambiguous teachings of an important religion" (*The Guardian* [London], June 4, 2004).

3. I refer here not to such recent incidents as the Oklahoma bombings but to something older and more deep-seated. For a hundred years after the ending of slavery in the United States, African Americans in the South lived in extreme fear. The primary instrument of this terror was the lynching by whites of alleged black murderers and rapists. Lynching was usually carried out in public and often involved ritualized torture. The historian Richard Maxwell Brown describes the crowds of spectators who assembled to witness such events, the pain and mutilation inflicted on the victims, and the perfunctory or nonexistent intervention by local law officers (*Strain of Violence: Historical Studies of American Violence and Vigilantism* [New York: Oxford University Press, 1975, esp. pp. 217–18.) In her detailed analysis of twelve hundred cases of blacks lynched by whites between 1882 and 1950, the sociologist Katherine Stovel labeled lynchings that incorporated ritual but did not take place before large crowds "terrorist lynchings" ("Local Sequential Patterns: The Structure of Lynching in the Deep South, 1882–1930," *Social Forces* 79, no. 3 [March 2001]: 855). This appellation is somewhat misleading, however, because virtually all such lynchings were demonstrative and therefore created terror in the black community. As Brown notes, "The entire lynching ritual was structured to give dramatic warning to all black inhabitants that the iron-clad system of white supremacy was not to be challenged by deed, word, or even thought" (*Strain of Violence*, p. 218). In this form of terrorism within a liberal democratic state, a racially privileged part of the population systematically terrorizes its racially stigmatized fellow citizens while the state stands apart. Although

lynchings have ceased, the social consequences of this violence are deeply embedded in the pattern of U.S. race relations today.

4. This underlies the classic theory of the Atonement, first expressed by the early church fathers and then revived by Martin Luther. See Gustaf Aulen, *Christus Victor: An Historical Study of the Three Main Types of the Idea of Atonement* (London: SPCK, 1931).

I. TERRORISM

1. www.whitehouse.gov/new/releases/2001/09/20010911-16.html, accessed June 22, 2005; italics added.

2. www.whitehouse.gov/news/releases/2001/09/20010912-4.html.

3. Alain Badiou, "Philosophical Considerations of Some Recent Facts," *Theory & Event* 6, no. 2 (2002). If it is objected that most modern nations have been forged, in one way or another, through war, it may be replied that the United States is unique in the fact that its recent (nineteenth-century) formation as a transcontinental state—involving genocidal wars against indigenous inhabitants, the conquest of the West, and a reinvention of itself through a brutal civil war—has morphed into a global ambition. It is certainly the case that the United States has made war in one part of the world or another under every president who has held office over the last sixty years.

4. According to Tomaž Mastnak,

> For Charlemagne and his contemporaries, as for their predecessors, the Saracens were no more than one group of enemies among many, and not the one that worried them most. The Carolingians waged wars against the Muslims, it is true, but they also maintained diplomatic relations with them. . . . In fact most of the Carolingians' warlike energies were directed at wars against the Lombards, Saxons, Avars, Normans, Danes, and Slavs—these were the "foreign peoples." . . . The Christians fought an amorphous multitude of *pagani, gentiles, infideles*, and *barbari*.
>
> (*Crusading Peace* [Berkeley: University of California Press, 2000], pp. 106-7)

5. Marcel Gauchet, *The Disenchantment of the World: A Political History of Religion* (Princeton: Princeton University Press, 1997), p. 15. Gauchet's main thesis is that Christianity—and only Christianity—bears with-

in itself the seeds of worldly autonomy, which, when it comes to fruition in atheistical modernity, does away with religion, the principle of an externally imposed destiny.

6. See the study by Youssef Courbage and Philippe Fargues entitled *Christians and Jews under Islam* (London: I. B. Tauris, 1997), which demonstrates that the position of non-Muslims in Muslim-majority societies deteriorated when there were hostile confrontations with Western powers.

7. George Packer, "Fighting Faiths," *New Yorker*, July 10 and 17, 2006, p. 97.

8. Richard Rorty, "Post-Democracy," *London Review of Books* 26, no. 7 (2004).

9. See the introduction to *From Max Weber*, ed. and trans. H. H. Gerth and C. Wright Mills (London: Routledge and Kegan Paul, 1948), pp. 71–72, where Weber's letters on this subject are cited.

10. Walzer is known for his attempt to revive the "just war" theory in a secular guise and his famous book on that theme, *Just and Unjust Wars* (New York: Basic, 1992) is, among other things, a condemnation of the Vietnam War.

11. Michael Walzer, *Arguing About War* (New Haven: Yale University Press, 2004), p. 51.

12. This is reflected in the contradictory arguments made in his earlier book, *Just and Unjust Wars*, to the effect that, on the one hand, only soldiers may be killed (p. 136) and that, on the other, the rule that civilians should not be killed does not apply as an absolute (p. 154). This contradiction is nowhere resolved.

13. David Kennedy, *The Dark Sides of Virtue: Reassessing International Humanitarianism* (Princeton: Princeton University Press, 2004), p. 265.

14. Raimondo Catanzaro, ed., *The Red Brigades and Left-Wing Terrorism in Italy* (London: Pinter, 1991), p. 130.

15. In *Israel's Holocaust and the Politics of Nationhood* (Cambridge: Cambridge University Press, 2005), Idith Zertal describes the ideological use made of those who survived the Nazi mass murders—that is, the symbolic identification of their traumatic experience with Israel as a nation-state. The nation's leaders were not content to point to the many victims who survived the genocidal experience and who now lived in Israel but went on to claim the Israeli state as the sym-

bolic survivor of that experience, as its historic fulfillment and re-demption. Among other things, this has enabled the Palestinians (failed resisters of Israeli state power, defeated enemies of the Zion-ist project) to be represented as the present representatives of Nazi exterminism.

16. Benny Morris, *Righteous Victims: A History of the Zionist-Arab Conflict, 1881–1999* (New York: Knopf, 1999); idem, "Survival of the Fittest," *Haaretz*, September 1, 2004; idem, "For the Record," *The Guardian*, January 14, 2004.

17. Henry Siegman, "The Killing Equation," *New York Review of Books*, February 9, 2006, pp. 18–19.

18. "British and US policy focused on the development of 'firebomb-ing.' Allied scientists built model Japanese and German towns and applied their minds to calculating wind patterns and the right mix of incendiary and high-explosive bombs to create annihilating, ty-phoon-like 'firestorms' in densely populated German and Japanese cities" (Hugo Slim, "Why Protect Civilians? Innocence, Immunity and Enmity in War," *International Affairs* 79, no. 3 [2003]: 490). For a memo-rable account of the air war against German cities, see W. G. Sebald, *On the Natural History of Destruction* (New York: Modern Library, 2004), esp., on the horrors of the raid against Hamburg, pp. 26–29.

19. States that are signatories to various international instruments—and that means most states in the contemporary world—are required to follow certain rules of engagement; to what extent both sides in a war actually do so is often a matter of contention. Outright win-ners are obviously in a better position to declare than the defeated are who has broken the rules of engagement and what to do about it. The United States, as the world's greatest power, appropriates to itself the right to judge its own military commanders in the matter. Although most countries in the world have not ratified the Inter-national Criminal Court statute, only the United States has deliber-ately tried to circumvent it. Apparently concerned that its soldiers or officials might be subject to prosecution for war crimes in the court, the USA has negotiated over ninety bilateral treaties ensuring that other countries do not surrender U.S. nationals to the ICC.

20. Antony Anghie, *Imperialism, Sovereignty and the Making of International Law* (Cambridge: Cambridge University Press, 2004), p. 278.

21. Brian Michael Jenkins, "The New Age of Terrorism," in David Kamien, ed., *The McGraw-Hill Homeland Security Handbook* (New York: McGraw-Hill, 2005), p. 117.
22. Joanna Bourke, *An Intimate History of Killing: Face-to-Face Killing in Twentieth-Century Warfare* (New York: Basic, 1999), p. 67.
23. In an unpublished paper entitled "Civil Liberties, Terrorism and Difference" (2006), Partha Chatterjee gives a fascinating account of the close connection between the definition of a legal-political space called terrorism and the processes of imperial rule in British India.
24. Richard A. Falkenrath (senior fellow at the Brookings Institute, former White House deputy, and Homeland Security adviser) in his foreword to *The MacGraw-Hill Homeland Security Handbook*. Falkenrath makes a strong plea for universities to take up the vital task of training such experts who can effectively address the problem of the new—and permanent—threat posed by terrorism.
25. In an interesting survey of U.S. "democracy promotion programs," William P. Alford observes: "Law has, in recent years, come to occupy an increasing role in democracy assistance because some proponents see it as promoting liberal values (at least in the minimal sense of fostering regularity, predictability, and constraints on the arbitrary exercise of state power). Paradoxically, however, a considerable number of democracy promotion advocates also tend to portray law as neutral and hence capable of being effectively deployed by a range of different regimes to achieve a broad spectrum of developmental ends" ("Exporting 'The Pursuit of Happiness,'" *Harvard Law Review* 113, no. 7 [2000]: 1708). According to this writer, the notion of "rule of law" is thus compatible with a variety of regimes—in the United States as well as abroad, in wartime and in peace.
26. I use "intention" to refer to the causal structure of a social act and "motive" to refer to the actor's reasons for acting in a particular way.
27. See Al Gore, "The Politics of Fear," *Social Research* 7, no. 4 (2004): 783.
28. The press, television, and popular books can also contribute here. Take, for example, Steven Emerson's *American Jihad: The Terrorists Living Among Us* (New York: Free, 2002). A recent *New York Times* best seller, it is described on the back cover as "The indispensable guide to American Muslim extremists and their ties to international terrorism." Why is such a guide indispensable? To help U.S. readers—the

more the better—uncover hidden dangers. Although the guide assimilates "militants" to "terrorists" and "anti-Americanism" to both, it also explains why these equations are semantically justified: "Yet if it is wrong to consider all Muslims terrorists, so is it wrong to assume that all Muslim militants carry automatic weapons, wear scruffy beards, and shout 'Death to America.' . . . It is precisely the Westernized intellectuals in Muslim countries who are most susceptible to anti-Americanism and Islamic militancy. The posture seems to represent, in part, a recoil from the stresses of trying to assimilate to another culture" (pp. 141–42). For Emerson, the absence of clear signs indicating the terrorist is itself an incitement to interpretation.

29. "Rhetoric of the Image," in *Image-Music-Text*, ed. and trans. Stephen Heath (London: Fontana, 1977), p. 39.

30. Found at www.gwu.edu/-nsarchiv/NSAEBB/NSAEBB122/, accessed February 18, 2005; printout in possession of the author. As a consequence of Congress investigations in the mid-1980s of reported atrocities in Central America, the manual posted on the Web was edited by hand to warn readers that the use of coercive techniques was illegal. According to Alfred McCoy, CIA-funded experiments carried out on psychiatric patients and prisoners in the 1950s helped develop techniques of "no-touch torture," including sensory deprivation and self-inflicted punishment (see especially chapter 2, "Mind Control," in *A Question of Torture: CIA Interrogation from the Cold War to the War on Terror* [New York: Henry Holt, 2006]).

31. This information is of two kinds: "1. Standing requirements—e.g. information concerning threats against government officials, subversive groups, terrorist actions, armed attack. 2. Specific requirements—e.g. information concerning a topic about which a subject has specialized knowledge, such as scientific or technical knowledge" (p. A-16).

32. The CIA manual also provides the interrogator with a list of "personality categories" of characters whose inner weaknesses can be traced through external signs. The types include: "The orderly-obstinate subject," "The optimistic subject," "The greedy, demarding subject," "The anxious self-centered subject," "The guilt-ridden subject," "The subject wrecked by success," "The schizoid subject," "The exception," and "The average or normal subject". Of this last, it is

observed that the subject "may exhibit most or all of the characteristics of the other categories from time to time" (pp. G-14 to G-111). All these categories, but especially the last, require a flexibility of judgment on the part of the interrogator and a manner that combines solicitousness with menace.

33. Graham Greene, *Our Man in Havana* (Harmondsworth: Penguin, 1962), pp. 150–51.

34. Cited in Rony Brauman, "Mission civilisatrice, ingérence humanitaire," in Pascal Blanchard, Nicolas Bancel, and Sandrine Lemaire, eds., *La Fracture coloniale: La société française au prisme de l'héritage colonial* (Paris: La Découverte, 2005), pp. 166–67. Rony Brauman shows that "compassion," as the given cause of Euro-American interventions in the "uncivilized" world, was always a highly politicized notion. See also Martti Koskenniemi, *The Gentle Civilizer of Nations: The Rise and Fall of International Law 1870–1960* (Cambridge: Cambridge University Press, 2001); and Anghie, *Imperialism, Sovereignty and the Making of International Law.*

35. Captain Elbridge Colby, "How to Fight Savage Tribes," *American Journal of International Law* 21, no. 2 (1927): 285.

36. "'We face an enemy that targets innocent civilians,' Gonzales would tell journalists two years later, at the height of the furor over the abuse of prisoners at Abu Ghraib prison in Iraq. 'We face an enemy that lies in the shadows, an enemy that doesn't sign treaties. They don't wear uniforms, an enemy that owes no allegiance to any country. They do not cherish life. An enemy that doesn't fight, attack or plan according to accepted laws of war, in particular [the] Geneva Conventions'" (Seymour M. Hersh, *Chain of Command: The Road from 9/11 to Abu Ghraib* [New York: HarperCollins, 2004], p. 5). Hersh, who has documented the details, is clearly outraged by this statement, but what I find more interesting is that the political and military establishment of the United States doesn't seem to share this outrage.

37. Jenkins, "The New Age of Terrorism," p. 118. In characterizing terrorist violence in these terms, Jenkins overlooks the enormous number of civilian deaths perpetrated by the U.S. military alone (in Afghanistan and Iraq), a number far greater than all recent terrorist killings put together.

38. Max Boot, *The Savage Wars of Peace: Small Wars and the Rise of American Power* (New York: Basic, 2003).

39. See, in this connection, Colonel C.E. Callwell's classic, *Small Wars: Their Principles and Practices* (London: H. M. Stationery Office, 1906), and the *Small Wars Manual: United States Marine Corps, 1940* (Washington, D.C.: U.S. Government Printing Office, 1940).

40. See Kenneth R. Rizer, "Bombing Dual-Use Targets: Legal, Ethical, and Doctrinal Perspectives," *Air and Space Power Chronicles*, May 2001, www.airpower.maxwell.af.mil/airchronicles/cc/Rizer.html.

41. Michael Walzer, "The Ethics of Battle: War Fair," *New Republic*, July 19, 2006, ssl.tnr.com/p/docsub.mhtml?i=20060731&s=walzer073106; printout in possession of the author. As a contribution to the ethics of battle, Walzer's statement is unimpressive; it makes no effort to argue against existing humanitarian law that explicitly contradicts his assertion. As a form of reasoning that aims at the disciplining of uncivilized populations, however, it is excellent. Incidentally, Walzer neglects to say that Hezbollah rockets fired into civilian areas of northern Israel were in direct response to Israel's massive bombing of civilian targets in southern Lebanon immediately after the Hezbollah capture of two soldiers. (See, for example, *The Guardian* of July 13–15 2006.) Nor does he mention that there is a long history of kidnapping by both Israel and Hezbollah specifically for the purpose of prisoner exchange. (See, for example, the Israel Ministry of Foreign Affairs Website on the abduction by Israeli commandos of Sheikh Abdul Karim Obeid, leader of Hezbollah, on July 28, 1989 [www.mfa.gov.il/MFA/Foreign+Relations/Israels+Foreign+Relations+since+1947/19. . . , accessed August 3, 2006].) A well-informed recent article on Hezbollah's role in the recent Lebanese-Israeli conflict is Charles Glass, "Learning from Mistakes," *London Review of Books* 28, no. 16 (August 17, 2006).

42. Oliver O'Donovan, *The Just War Revisited* (Cambridge: Cambridge University Press, 2003), p. 64.

43. Zbigniew Brzezinski, "American Strategy and the Middle East," talk given in Washington, D.C., July 20, 2006, www.thewashingtonnote.com/archives/Brzezinksi%20speech%207-20web.htm, accessed August 3, 2006.

44. Walzer, "The Ethics of Battle."
45. Colby, "How to Fight Savage Tribes," p. 287; my emphasis.

2. SUICIDE TERRORISM

1. Jean Baechler, *Suicides* (New York: Basic, 1979), p. 36 and p. 409 ff.
2. Baechler dismisses a range of familiar definitions and comes up with the following: "Suicide denotes all behavior that seeks and finds the solution to an existential problem by making an attempt on the life of the subject" (ibid., p. 11).
3. Jon Elster, "Motivations and Beliefs in Suicide Missions," in Diego Gambetta, ed., *Making Sense of Suicide Missions* (Oxford: Oxford University Press, 2005), p. 240. Elster goes on to propose that "such trance-like states most likely do not spring from a stable motivational system" (p. 240).
4. Explanations included "total misfits rejected by other pupils," "exposure to violent video games," "seeking attention," and so on, all of which turned out to be factually incorrect, or speculative, or tautological. The massacre was the central incident in Michael Moore's movie *Bowling for Columbine* and in another feature movie modeled on the event, Gus Van Sant's *Elephant*. Moore used the slaughter emblematically to make the uncontentious point that fear and violence are endemic to American culture.
5. Ivan Strenski, "Sacrifice, Gift and the Social Logic of Muslim Human Bombers," in *Terrorism and Political Violence* 15, no. 3 (2003): 8.
6. Ibid., p. 21.
7. May Jayyusi, "Subjectivity and Public Witness: An Analysis of Islamic Militance in Palestine," unpublished paper for the SSRC Beirut Conference on the Public Sphere in the Middle East, October 2004.
8. The full passage in Arendt reads as follows:

> Rage is by no means an automatic reaction to misery and suffering as such.... Only where there is reason to suspect that conditions could be changed and are not does rage arise. Only when our sense of justice is offended do we react with rage, and this reaction by no means necessarily reflects personal injury.... To resort to violence when confronted with outrageous events or conditions is enormously tempting because of its

inherent immediacy and swiftness. . . . The point is that under certain circumstances—acting without argument or speech and *without counting the
consequences*—is the only way to set the scales of justice right again. (Billy
Budd, striking dead the man who bore false witness against him, is the
classic example.) In this sense, rage and the violence that sometimes—not
always—goes with it belong among the "natural" *human* emotions, and to
cure man of them would mean nothing less than to dehumanize or emas-
culate him.

(Hannah Arendt, *On Violence* [London: Allen Lane, 1969],
pp. 63–64, italics in original)

9. If by "individuation" Jayyusi means recognizing the individual as the
subject of will and responsibility, then it is not clear why she thinks
this is a new development. In Islamic doctrine, the concepts of will
and responsibility have always been present.

10. The Qur'anic verse cited here (3:169) is conventionally interpreted
as a reference to martyrdom but the word for "martyr," *shahīd*, does
not appear there. The verse actually refers to *alladhīna qutilū fī sabīl
illāhi*—"those who have been killed in God's cause." The passive form
allows Palestinians to cite it in the context of the deaths of noncom-
batant civilians at the hands of the Israeli army.

11. Because she befriended Palestinians in the Jenin refugee camp during the intifada, Tali Fahima, a young Israeli Jewish woman, was
tried in Israel in 2005 for "giving aid to the enemy in times of war."
During this period, the portrait of Tali was stuck on the camp walls.
Tali's picture had the same honorific title as the portraits of Palestinian "martyrs." See Stéphanie Le Bars, "Tali Fahima, une Israélienne
trop curieuse," in *Le Monde*, September 24, 2005.

12. Ignaz Goldziher, *Muslim Studies*, ed. and trans. S. M. Stern (London:
Allen and Unwin, 1971), 2:351–52. The passage I cite is preceded by
this perplexity: "But it is remarkable that the meaning of the word
shahīd received an extension which is scarcely to be reconciled with
the warlike tendency of Islām." This does not, however, lead Goldziher to ask whether the notion of Islam's warlike tendency needs to
be reexamined. Nor does he explain why thinking in terms of the ad
hoc extension of an original meaning is preferable to regarding the
meanings as elements of a single semantic field.

13. Bruno Étienne, *Les combattants suicidaires* (Paris: Éditions de l'aube, 2005), p. 34.

14. Étienne doesn't mention the Hindu Tamil Tigers in Sri Lanka, who are said to have invented suicide bombing and who have claimed responsibility for more than two hundred and sixty bombings over the last two decades—averaging almost one a month—killing and injuring thousands, mostly civilians. "Of course we use suicide bombers," a Tiger official remarked to an American journalist, "because, as a revolutionary organization, we have limited resources" (Philip Gourevitch, "Letter From Sri Lanka: Tides of War," *New Yorker*, August 1, 2005, p. 56). By now (2006), Iraqi suicide bombings must have surpassed the Tamil record.

15. Sigmund Freud, *Totem and Taboo*.

16. R. Money-Kyrle, *The Meaning of Sacrifice* (London: Hogarth, 1929).

17. Étienne, *Les combattants suicidaires*, pp. 21–22.

18. Expressions such as "the Kingdom of God," "the Redeemer will triumph over the Beast," "those who have testified [*shuhadā*, from the root *shahāda*] will sit on the right hand of the father" are foreign to Islamic discourse—just as the Christian concept of "sacrifice" is. But they litter Étienne's text. The assumption that they are part of an authoritarian worldview shared by the monotheistic religions and can therefore help explain the *jihādist* project—assuming there is such a thing as a single clear project—seems to me unpersuasive.

19. See, for example, *Qur'ān karīm bi tafsīr al-imāmayn al-jalālayn jalāl ad-dīn muhammad al-mahallī wa jalāl ad-dīn as-suyūtī* (Damascus: Maktabat al-Mallah. 1978), pp. 256–57.

20. In classical Arabic, incidentally, the word *istishhād* meant "requiring someone to give evidence as in a court of law"; the standard word for "death while fighting in God's cause" was—and still is—*shahāda*. In the Islamic tradition, as in medieval Christian texts, *shahāda* is formally distinguished from suicide, *qatl an-nafs*—the modern Arabic word being *intihār*.

21. Étienne, *Les combattants suicidaires*, p. 17.

22. See WHO Regional Office for Europe, "Changing Patterns in Suicide Behaviour," *EURO Reports and Studies*, vol. 74 (Copenhagen, 1982), cited in Nadia Taysir Dabbagh, *Suicide in Palestine: Narratives of Despair* (London: Hurst, 2005), p. 10.

23. Étienne, *Les combattants suicidaires*, pp. 17–18.

24. Étienne is often perceptive but unconvincing in his attempt to treat the cruel civil war in Algeria and the suicide operations in Palestine as aspects of a single problem, to equate Christian apocalyptic discourse with the language of Islamic militants, and to treat *jihād* as virtually equivalent to *istishhād*. Freud's notion of thanatos against eros doesn't help in the problem Étienne has set himself: Freud proposed that since everything living dies for internal reasons (dissolves and becomes inorganic once again) "the aim of all life is death" and so death constitutes a return to the origin (Sigmund Freud, *Beyond the Pleasure Principle* (Standard Edition) [New York: Norton, 1961], pp. 45–46). Whatever else may be made of this idea, it cannot explain why suicide operations take place in particular times and places. In fact, Étienne's focus on Islamic violence as a syndrome requiring special explanation diverts the reader from attending to the centrality of violence and killing in all politics—including the politics that liberals themselves value and defend.

25. Robert A. Pape, "Dying to Kill Us," *New York Times*, September 22, 2003. Pape has elaborated his position in the form of a book: *Dying to Win: The Strategic Logic of Suicide Terrorism* (New York: Random House, 2005). This contains much interesting information, but the argument is essentially the same as the one advanced in the article.

26. Jayyusi, "Subjectivity and Public Witness."

27. Roxanne Euben, "Killing (for) Politics: Jihad, Martyrdom, Political Action," *Political Theory* 30, no. 1 (2002), 9.

28. The assumption that *jihādis* have a single motivation—and are involved in a single project—is widely shared by many. Thus the French expert on political Islam Olivier Roy, commenting on the July 7 London terror attacks, assumes that all acts of terror carried out by Muslim militants, from New York to Bali, are attributable to an organization called al-Qaeda. Roy even includes the murder of Theo van Gogh by a Dutch-born Muslim in his list of al-Qaeda atrocities and argues that the terrorism perpetrated by al-Qaeda has nothing to do with such things as U.S. interventions, Iraq, or Israel but with a determination "to provoke a clash of cultures" on a global scale. In my opinion, Roy is too hasty in drawing such conclusions. Consider the following points in his argument: (1) the al-Qaeda attacks of Septem-

ber 11 preceded the U.S. invasions of Afghanistan and Iraq (but was
U.S. military, economic, and political intervention in the region absent before 2001?); (2) the U.S. military base in Saudi Arabia has been
removed without this affecting al-Qaeda hostility to the Saudi regime (but has the military, economic, and security alliance between
the United States and the Saudi rulers been dissolved together with
the base?); (3) al-Qaeda published statements barely mention Israel
(in fact, several do—but does their concern with Israeli suppression
of Palestinians require that al-Qaeda mention it in every proclamation?); (4) the insurgents in Iraq have no political aim, not even the
establishment of an Islamic state (but are attacks against a foreign
occupier—and its perceived collaborators—not a political aim?); (5)
the Spanish police have discovered attacks planned by al-Qaeda
after the withdrawal of Spanish troops from Iraq (perhaps—but is
every plot uncovered by the police a plot by al-Qaeda?). Roy's assumptions do not prove that al-Qaeda is a central command center
responsible for acts of terror carried out throughout the world rather
than a source of inspiration for diffuse networks of militants who
believe they have grievances against the United States and its allies.
(See, incidentally, the excellent introduction by Bruce Lawrence to
his collection of pronouncements by Osama bin Laden: *Messages to
the World* [London: Verso, 2005].) That Muslim militants see the matter in terms of a global confrontation between a dominant United
States and its allies, on the one hand, and Islam, on the other, is true
(indeed, the United States is a global power, and it *does* deal with
those it sees as friends and enemies across the world), but all atrocities committed by Muslims do not add up to a single deadly motive.
In what sense, for example, did van Gogh's murderer, "avenging an
insult to Islam," and the London bombers, attacking ordinary Brit-
ishers "for the war in Iraq," have the same motive? (See Roy's piece
in *Le Monde Diplomatique*, English edition, August 2005.)
29. Euben, "Killing (for) Politics," p. 22.
30. Ibid., p. 27.
31. The best-known (and most persuasive) statement of this view is
Robert Cover's *Narrative, Violence, and the Law* (Ann Arbor: University
of Michigan Press, 1992).

32. Richard Tuck, *The Rights of War and Peace: Political Thought and International Order from Grotius to Kant* (Oxford: Oxford University Press, 1999), p. 195.

33. Although why the liberal autonomous individual would continue indefinitely to be bound by the original act of delegation even when his self-interest dictates otherwise is not clear. Of course, the constituted state has awesome sanctions—coercive and manipulative—at its disposal to make him obey, but then his obedience is no longer a simple consequence of the social contract.

34. See Antony Anghie, *Imperialism, Sovereignty and the Making of International Law* (Cambridge: Cambridge University Press, 2004), chap. 6.

35. Ibid., p. 294.

36. Thus Seymour Hersh: "Israeli field commanders have accepted nuclear artillery shells and land mines as battlefield necessities. . . . The basic target of Israel's nuclear arsenal has been and will continue to be its Arab neighbors. Should war break out in the Middle East again and should the Syrians and the Egyptians break through again as they did in 1973 [Yom Kippur War], or should any Arab nation fire missiles again at Israel, as Iraq did [in the 1991 Gulf War], a nuclear escalation, once unthinkable except as a last resort, would now be a strong possibility" (*The Samson Option: Israel's Nuclear Arsenal and American Foreign Policy* [New York: Random House, 1991], p. 319).

37. To these might be added the depleted uranium shells and white phosphorous that have been used by the U.S. forces in the Iraq war.

38. John Keegan, *The Face of Battle* (Harmondsworth, U.K.: Penguin, 1978), pp. 329–30; my italics in the last sentence.

39. Margaret Canovan, "On Being Economical with the Truth: Some Liberal Reflections," *Political Studies* 38 (1990): 16.

40. Michael Walzer, *Arguing About War* (New Haven: Yale University Press, 2004), p. 45.

3. HORROR AT SUICIDE TERRORISM

1. The number of books devoted to this subject is already very considerable, and they deal with a familiar range of explanations—essentially those I have discussed in my second chapter. Here are just

a few that I have read in addition to those mentioned in previous chapters: Terry McDermott, *Perfect Soldiers: The Hijackers—Who They Were, Why They Did It* (New York: HarperCollins, 2005); Anne Marie Oliver and Paul F. Steinberg, *The Road to Martyrs Square: A Journey into the World of the Suicide Bomber* (Oxford: Oxford University Press, 2005); Ami Pedahzur, *Suicide Terrorism* (Cambridge: Polity, 2005); Mia Bloom, *Dying to Kill: The Allure of Suicide Terror* (New York: Columbia University Press, 2005); Farhad Khosrokhavar, *Suicide Bombers: Allah's New Martyrs* (London: Pluto, 2002); Raphel Israeli, *Islamekaze: Manifestations of Islamic Martyrology* (London: Cass, 2003); Lauri S. Friedman, *What Motivates Suicide Bombers?* (Detroit: Greenhaven, 2005); Christoph Reuter, *My Life Is a Weapon: A Modern History of Suicide Bombing* (Princeton: Princeton University Press, 2004); Joyce Davis, *Martyrs: Innocence, Vengeance, and Despair in the Middle East* (New York: Palgrave Macmillan, 2003); and Rosemarie Skaine, *Female Suicide Bombers* (Jefferson, N.C.: McFarland, 2006). In this literature, suicide bombers are a recognizable type. Even the distinguished author John Updike has moved into this territory with his latest novel *Terrorist* (New York: Knopf, 2005)—a tale set in urban America, complete with fanatical Arab sheikhs and more human American converts to Islam.

2. Jacqueline Rose, "Deadly Embrace," *London Review of Books* 26, no. 21 (November 4, 2004).

3. The majority of Muslims have tended to regard even the deliberate seeking of martyrdom (*talab al-shahāda*) as prohibited. See, for example, Abu Hamid Muhammad bin Muhammad al-Ghazali, *Ihya 'ulūmaddin*, 5 vols. (Beirut: Dar al-Kutub al-'Ilmiya, 2001), 2:285–86, the most famous work of perhaps the most influential medieval Muslim theologian in history. Today, this position is also that of the Wahhabis of Saudi Arabia. Both their eighteenth-century founder, Muhammad bin Abdul-Wahhab (see Muhammad bin Abdul Wahhab, *Mu'allafāt al-shaykh al-imām Muhammad bin 'abdalwahhab*, vol. 2, *al-Fiqh* [Riyadh: Islamic University, n.d.], pp. 3 ff.), and the leading Saudi theologians today have condemned suicide of any kind as sinful. In an interview several months before the attack on the World Trade Center but after the first suicide bombings in Israel, the Saudi grand mufti, Shaykh Abd al-Aziz bin Abdallah Al al-Shaykh, declared all

terrorism (*tarwī'*) legally forbidden (see "*Muftī 'āmm al-sa'ūdiyya li-l-sharq al-awsat: Khatf al-tā'irāt wa tarwī' al-āminīn muharram shar'an,*" in the daily *al-Sharq al-awsat,* April 21, 2001). According to the shaykh, while *jihād* was enjoined in Islam, suicide (*intihār*) could under no circumstances be regarded as permitted. Other muftis, such as the Egyptian Yusuf al-Qaradawi, have taken a contrary view in the case of Palestinian suicide bombings.

4. Not all judicial self-executions were private: the ceremonial suicide known as hara-kiri (seppuku) in nineteenth-century Japan was conducted in the presence of a large assembly. See the first European description of one such suicide in *Tales of Old Japan,* by Lord Redesdale (A. B. Freeman-Mitford), published in London by Macmillan in 1910.

5. According to al-Sha'rāwi, one of the most influential preachers in the Arabic-speaking world, suicide is to be classed together with madness and is (tautologically) a sign of loss of faith in God. That is why, he says, it is more common in the unbelieving West. (See Muhammad Mutawally al-Sha'rāwi, *Al-fatāwa al-kubra* [Beirut: al-Maktaba al-'asriyya, 2005], pp. 97, 103–4.) Thus whereas in antiquity suicide could be an honorable completion to life, here it is a sign of supreme irrationality. This view is, of course, found in all the Abrahamic religions, but the idea of suicide as an act of supreme unreason is also very strong in secular law and morality.

6. Stanley Cavell, *The Claim of Reason* (New York: Oxford University Press, 1999), pp. 418–19.

7. News story by Craig Nelson in the *Atlanta Journal-Constitution,* September 14, 2003, p. 5A.

8. Nadelson cites the passage from the *Iliad* in which Patroclus kills a Trojan with his spear, like catching a fish:

There is joy and celebration of the killer's own life, skillfully taking a life. He is the hunter or, in the simile, the fisherman, the superior of the slain, the quick not the dead. He is the manifest lord raised high by the dead body he has created. The victim is face down, neutered, dirtied, and diminished. The killer has manifested the most naked self-assertion. He is lasciviousness personified. He is adulated as a hero, his potency glorified; he shines. The el-

egance of killing action in war is celebrated throughout the Greek tragedies;
it is echoed in the Hebrew Bible . . . and in literature on war through history.

(Theodore Nadelson, *Trained to Kill: Soldiers at War*
[Baltimore: Johns Hopkins University Press, 2005], p. 64)

9. Ibid., pp. 68–69.

10. Ibid.

11. Like Lester Farley in Philip Roth's *The Human Stain* (New York: Vintage, 2000), a highly disturbed veteran who cannot understand why in Vietnam he was trained and encouraged to kill the enemy ("And all he did was what they trained him to do: you see the enemy, you kill the enemy" [p. 69]) but when he tried to do just that in his home he was put into leather restraints and sedated.

12. Dave Grossman, *On Killing: The Psychological Cost of Learning to Kill in War and Society* (New York: Little, Brown, 1995), p. 75.

13. Blindness is often depicted in rabbinical literature as punishment for sin according to the divine principle of measure for measure: "Samson went after [the desire of] his eyes—therefore the Philistines put out his eyes, as it is written, *And the Philistines laid hold on him and put out his eyes* (Judg. 16: 21)"—cited in Martha Himmelfarb, *Tours of Hell, An Apocalyptic Form in Jewish and Christian Literature* (Philadelphia: University of Pennsylvania Press, 1983), p. 77.

14. Shortly after the attack on the World Trade Center, Karlheinz Stockhausen described it in awe as "a work of art." See the unsigned article "Attacks Called Great Art," *New York Times*, September 19, 2001. The anger this occasioned led him to protest that he had been misunderstood.

15. F. T. Prince, introduction to Milton's *Samson Agonistes* (Oxford: Oxford University Press, 1957), p. 17. Prince's own poems (of which the most famous is "Soldiers Bathing") are exquisite celebrations of suffering as an aesthetic—even erotic—experience.

16. Samson's farewell message to his scattered and oppressed people consists of threefold advice: collect iron (weapons), choose a king (an absolute leader), and learn to laugh (be fearless). See Z. Jabotinsky, *Samson* (New York: Judaea, 1986), translated from the German translation of the Russian, first published 1927. (The novel was also used as a source for the script of the 1949 Hollywood blockbuster

Samson and Delilah.) For Zionists, the Bible is, of course, much more than a religious text; it is also a national charter. All the founders of Israel sought to create "a new Jew" in place of the old European stereotypes, but the revisionist Jabotinsky was particularly concerned to reconstruct the Jew as warrior, as strong, fearless, and uncompromising toward his enemies. That, for Jabotinsky and his ideological descendents, is "the real Jew," the original Jew of biblical times.

17. David Grossman, *Lion's Honey: The Myth of Samson* (London: Cannongate, 2006). In her excellent review of this book, Jenny Diski rightly questions the assimilation of the state with the psyche of the individual; see "Heaps Upon Heaps," in *London Review of Books* 28, no. 14 (July 2006).

18. Mary Douglas, *Purity and Danger: An Analysis of Concepts of Pollution and Taboo* (London: Routledge and Kegan Paul, 1966).

19. Franz Steiner, *Taboo* (London: Cohen and West, 1958).

20. See the excellent article by Marc Berthod, "Mort et vif: Penser le statut paradoxal des défunts," in S. Chappaz-Wirthner, A. Monsutti, and O. Schinz, eds., *Entre ordre et subversion: Logiques plurielles, alternatives, écarts, paradoxes* (Paris: Karthala, 2006).

21. Georges Bataille, *The Tears of Eros*, trans. Peter Connor (San Francisco: City Lights, 1989), pp. 205–7.

22. Susan Sontag, commenting on Bataille's statement about the photograph, writes that

Bataille is not saying that he takes pleasure at the sight of this excruciation. But he is saying that he can imagine extreme suffering as something more than just suffering, as a kind of transfiguration. It is a view of suffering, of the pain of others, that is rooted in religious thinking, which links pain to sacrifice, sacrifice to exaltation—a view that could not be more alien to a modern sensibility, which regards suffering as something that is a mistake or an accident or a crime. Something to be fixed. Something to be refused. Something that makes one feel powerless.

(*Regarding the Pain of Others* [New York: Farrar, Straus and Giroux, 2003], pp. 98–99)

She fails to note, however, that the modern sensibility is contradictory: the endurance of suffering is to be refused but inflicting suffering on others (judicial punishment and war being obvious examples) is not.

23. Adam Lowenstein, *Shocking Representation: Historical Trauma, National Cinema, and the Modern Horror Film* (New York: Columbia University Press, 2005), p. 22.

24. When I first saw *Le sang des bêtes* in the early nineties, like others, I was horrified, but I made no connection with the industrial killing of the Holocaust. The critic may say I saw it naively. But my claim is not that I made a correct reading of the film; it is that I engaged with it viscerally: *that* and not interpretation was the basis of horror *and delight* (in Burke's sense).

25. Stuart Klawans, "Cruel and Unusual Punishment," *The Nation*, January 30, 2006.

26. Simone de Beauvoir, *Force of Circumstance*, trans. Richard Howard (New York: Putnam, 1965), p. 656.

27. In a compelling article on Franz Kafka's "The Metamorphosis," Martin Greenberg writes that the story is about death "but death that is without denouement, death that is merely a spiritually inconclusive petering out" ("Gregor Samsa and Modern Spirituality," in Harold Bloom, ed., *Franz Kafka's The Metamorphosis* [New York: Chelsea House, 1988], p. 19). The story does not symbolize death, it simply traces a dying that has no meaning. This observation helps to explain the story's capacity to shock: both the inevitability of a secular emptying out and Samsa's realization that how others see him is utterly different from what he takes himself to be together undermine any attempt to account for his status as a human being.

28. E. E. Evans-Pritchard, deploying a Christian idea in the interpretation of an African religion, once remarked that, "in sacrifice, then, some part of a man dies with the victim. It can be regarded both as an absolution and a rebirth; and also as self-immolation (the psycho-analysts use the word 'suicide')" (*Nuer Religion* [Oxford: Clarendon, 1956], p. 281). (The reference to "psycho-analysis" is to R. Money-Kyrle's study on sacrifice, mentioned in my second chapter.) This Christian complex of partial death, absolution, and rebirth is absent in the Islamic tradition of sacrifice. The reference to dying as partial, however, may at first sight appear to be mere metaphor, but it can be argued that this is only so if one insists on taking death as the binary opposite of life. The recent biomedical concept of brain death

and the practice of organ transplantation have begun to complicate this simple binary at a biological level.

29. See Timothy Gorringe, *God's Just Vengeance* (Cambridge: Cambridge University Press, 1996). Gorringe takes his distance from the punitive model of the Crucifixion that has been dominant throughout Christian history and offers instead a humanist interpretation that is friendly to liberal penal policies.

30. Thus the legal sentence of "life in solitary confinement" arouses no noticeable liberal criticism, although prisoners are permanently isolated in their cells with only two hours a day to wander in a small yard where they can see the sky through a narrow opening. "Time takes its toll and they just rot," said one penal expert with evident satisfaction ("'Supermax' for Worst of Worst," *New York Post*, May 4, 2006, p. 4).

31. John 13:21–28.

32. In his study of medieval attitudes to violence, the art historian Valentin Groebner writes:

> How we look at crucifixes nowadays differs from how people did so five centuries ago. One could say with equal justification that the Crucified also looks at *us* differently. After all, the visual culture of Europe and America is deeply marked by the figure of a bloody male body as a representation of truth. Imaginations of human faces rendered violently misshapen remain effective at the beginning of the twenty-first century. To this day, moral tales are frequently organized around the body of a bloodied man as a figure of truth. In contrast to images of abused women, the image of a naked wounded male body in films evokes not sexual but morally lofty connotations.
>
> (*Defaced: The Visual Culture of Violence in the Late Middle Ages*
> [New York: Zone, 2004], pp. 121–22)

Groebner rightly notes the sexism in such visual representations, but he does not explore how the wounded male hero standing for truth can himself be an object of passionate love in the eye of the spectator.

33. A recent (2006) example is the widely acclaimed film *Syriana*, in which the CIA agent—played by George Clooney—survives torture by an Arab and moves on to the slow discovery of truth. Many

contemporary Arab regimes have skilled torturers at their dispos-
able, but an American hero tortured on the screen by an Arab is certainly a neat conceit in the age of Abu Ghraib.

34. Richard Gamble, *The War for Righteousness: Progressive Christianity, the
Great War, and the Rise of the Messianic Nation* (Wilmington, Del.: ISI,
2003), p. 5.

35. Cited in ibid., p. 153.

36. As James Marrow observes,

> One of the best-known aspects of the piety of the late Middle Ages is the
> rise of devotion to the suffering Christ. The desire of pious men and women
> to approach the divine through intimate knowledge and empathic expe-
> rience of Christ's humanity and Passion led to profound developments
> in religious literature and art: content and style underwent evolutionary
> changes mirroring the humanized and emotional religiosity of the period,
> and entirely new genres were created, for example, Passion Plays, and the
> visual representations known as *Andachtsbilder*, or devotional images.
>> ("Circumdederunt me canes multi: Christ's Tormentors in Northern
>> European Art of the Late Middle Ages and Early Renaissance,"
>> Art Bulletin 59 [1977]: 167).

See also Paul Binski, *Medieval Death: Ritual and Representation* (Ithaca,
N.Y.: Cornell University Press, 1990), for the development of sensibilities connecting inner veneration with compassion for the physical
sufferings endured by Christ and the saints.

37. Jacques Le Goff, *Medieval Civilization* (Oxford: Blackwell, 1988), p. 158.
For his general account of the ways in which the figure of Christ
crucified entered into and modulated medieval devotion and sensibility, see especially pp. 152–59. See also Jan Huizinga, *The Waning
of the Middle Ages* (Harmondsworth: Penguin, 1955), for more on the
intertwining between cruelty and compassion.

38. For example, the fifteenth-century guide on how to live a devout
Christian life, *Opera a ben vivere*, written by the archbishop of Flor-
ence, who was also a friend of the painter Fra Angelico, urges that

> you should meditate a little every day on the passion of our Lord Jesus
> Christ. . . . Kneel down before a Crucifix and with the eyes of the mind,
> more than with those of the body, consider his face. Beginning first with

the crown of thorns, pressed into his head, down to his skull; next the eyes, full of tears and of blood; the mouth, frothing and full of bile and blood; the beard, similarly full of spit and of blood and of bile. . . . And in reverence of all these things, you should recite the Lord's prayer with a Hail Mary.

> (cited in Laurence Kanter and Pia Palladino, *Fra Angelico* [New Haven: Yale University Press, 2005], p. 174)

The authors point to Angelico's famous *Christ Crowned with Thorns*, which contains these gruesome details.

39. Laurinda Dixon, *Bosch* (London: Phaidon, 2003), p. 121.
40. It will be recalled that Ernest Renan's famous essay "What Is a Nation" ends with a paean to the importance of suffering in unifying the nation: "La nation, comme l'individu, est l'aboutissant d'un long passé d'efforts, de sacrifices et de dévouements. . . . On aime en proportion des sacrifices qu'on a consentis, des maux qu'on a soufferts. . . . Oui, la souffrance en commun unit plus que la joie" (*Qu'est-ce qu'une nation?* [Paris: Presses Pocket, 1992], p. 54). Clearly, war is a central site of sacrifice in Renan's scheme, necessary to the persistence of the nation. Theodore Nadelson, whom I cited earlier, puts it more bluntly:

> That we must wage war for civilization is clear; it seems we must fight and kill for our self-preservation. The veterans made me realize that I could still feel the rage available to kill those who came to kill me and mine. Now I see the available rage as necessary for maintaining our own civilization. The events of September 11, 2001, underscored that. We persist as a nation and as a civilization only because we have often fought mortal battles for our preservation. Our arts, laws, and science as part of our civilization continue, not because of their many virtues, but because we also have the moral will to defend them—and now the battle is against a fundamentalist faction of Islam whose unshakeable dogma is restriction without debate, intolerance, and the demeaning of women.
>
> (*Trained to Kill*, p. 169)

41. C. John Sommerville, *The Decline of the Secular University* (New York: Oxford University Press, 2006), p. 59.

42. See the interesting study by Adrian Caesar, *Taking It Like a Man: Suffering, Sexuality and the War Poets* (Manchester, U.K.: Manchester University Press, 1993), where the statement I cite occurs at p. 234.

43. "Transplant's hailed technological advancements also generate perplexing ethical questions that dog medical professionals," writes Lesley Sharp.

> Human organs are regularly subjected to elaborate metaphorical reworking that ultimately silences such unease. The most pervasive and obvious example involves relabeling organs as "gifts of life," a process that quickly mystifies the economic realities of their origins. Within the United States, transplantable organs must be given willingly, unselfishly, and anonymously, and any money that is exchanged is to be perceived as being solely for operational costs, but never for the organs themselves. To request or offer any form of monetary compensation tears at the very fabric of American (and, in effect, assumed Judeo-Christian) ideals surrounding altruism where one quite literally gives oneself to others in need.
>
> ("Commodified Kin: Death, Mourning, and Competing Claims on the Bodies of Organ Donors in the United States," *American Anthropologist* 103, no. 1 (March 2001): 116)

Sharp describes how anonymity is closely linked to a growing market in the supply and demand of organs. See also Nancy Scheper-Hughes, "The Global Traffic in Human Organs," *Current Anthropology* 41, no. 2 (2000).

44. For an excellent study on this subject, see Margaret Lock, *Twice Dead: Organ Transplants and the Reinvention of Death* (Berkeley: University of California Press, 2002).

45. The first Palestinian suicide attack in Israel took place in revenge for an Israeli extrajudicial killing of a Hamas official in 1994.

46. Emile Durkheim, *The Division of Labor in Society*, trans. George Simpson (Glencoe, Ill.: Free, 1960). See especially chapter 2.

EPILOGUE

1. The interview is cited in Yasmin Alibhai Brown, "Opinion," *The Independent*, July 17, 2006, p. 29.

INDEX

INDEX COMPILED BY FRED LEISE

of, 2; implicit association of Muslims with, 1; models for discussion of, 15; religious terrorism, 1, 8–9, 45; responses to, terms used for, 8; and vulnerability, feelings of, 26; Walzer's views on, 16, 22. *See also* cruelty; suicide terrorism; violence; war on terror

terrorists: motives of, vs. insurgents', 36–37; soldiers, comparison with, 25–26

torturables vs. untorturables, 32–33

torture: no-touch, 103n30; of prisoners, in military training, 28; torturables vs. untorturables, 32–33; use in war against terrorism, 17; and war/terrorism distinction, 31–32

Traité de psychologie (Dumas), 79

Tuck, Richard, 59

umma (just community of Muslims), 57

uncertain signs, 31

uncivilized nations, vs. civilized, 34, 38

United States: Hussein, support for, 13; International Criminal Court and, 101n19; Iraq, effects of invasion of, 14; as locus for war on terror, 2; Middle East, interventionist tradition in, 13; Muslims in, effects of September 11, 2001 on, 1; official hermeneutics in,

31; Patriot Act, 30; torture, use of, 33; wars by, 99n3

Updike, John, 112n1

vengeance, 90

Vietnam War, 71–72

violence: incomprehensibility of, 8; legitimate violence, 3; in military training, 27–28; in modern age, 86; politics and, 17, 59; as precondition to politics, 58; space of, 28–29; states and, 29. *See also* cruelty; terrorism

Walzer, Michael, 15–20, 22–26; on allowable evil, 18–19; on civilian deaths, 36; on coercion, 19; criticisms of, 105n41; on emergency ethics, 18; on guilt, 17–18; on humanitarianism, limitations to, 16–17; on Israel/Palestine conflict, 22–24; just war theory of, 100n10; on legal war, 16; on morally strong leaders, 17–18; states, dismissal of, 19; on terrorism, cause of, 17; on war, conditions for, 19

War Against Terrorism, 8

War in Vietnam, 71–72

War of Independence (Israel), 25

war on terror, 2, 22, 31–32

war poetry, 88

war(s): as category, logical criteria for, 39; colonial, 35–36; conscience in, 26; deaths from vs. from suicide bombing, 65–66;